Katy Perry

NOAM FRIEDLANDER

STERLING
New York

STERLING
New York

An Imprint of Sterling Publishing
387 Park Avenue South
New York, NY 10016

ISBN 978-1-4549-0364-2

Distributed in Canada by Sterling Publishing
c/o Canadian Manda Group, 165 Dufferin Street
Toronto, Ontario, Canada M6K 3H6
Distributed in the United Kingdom by GMC Distribution Services
Castle Place, 166 High Street, Lewes, East Sussex, England BN7 1XU
Distributed in Australia by Capricorn Link (Australia) Pty. Ltd.
P.O. Box 704, Windsor, NSW 2756, Australia

Produced for Sterling Publishing by Essential Works
www.essentialworks.co.uk

Publishing Director: Mal Peachey
Managing Director: John Conway
Editor: Nicola Hodgson
Designer: Michael Gray

Noam Friedlander would like to thank Michelle Jannone and Louise Griffiths.

For information about custom editions, special sales, and premium
and corporate purchases, please contact Sterling Special Sales
at 800-805-5489 or specialsales@sterlingpublishing.com.

Manufactured in China

10   9   8   7   6   5   4   3   2   1

Contents

Introduction   7

1 Being Katy Hudson   13

2 Becoming Katy Perry   29

3 I Kissed a Girl   49

4 Hello Katy   73

5 Baby You're a Firework   103

6 California Dreams   133

Credits   160

Introduction

Katy Perry is known today as a major recording artist, style icon, and worldwide sensation. It was through her tenacious perseverance and work ethic that she achieved true global domination.

Katheryn Elizabeth Hudson, who would later become known to the world as Katy Perry, was born on October 25, 1984, in Santa Barbara, California, to Christian pastor parents Keith and Mary Hudson. A scrawny tomboy with dark blond hair, "Katy Bird," as she was affectionately known within the family, grew up with an older sister, Angela, and a younger brother, David. The kids spent their childhoods traveling around the United States with their parents as they founded new churches. The family later settled back in Santa Barbara, where Katy spent her teenage years.

The Hudson siblings lived a sheltered life growing up. Katy's parents had strict beliefs and practices, and Christianity played a huge part in Katy Perry's upbringing and childhood. The family would read the Bible together—it was one of the few books her parents approved of and could trust the children alone with. Other aspects of popular culture, including television, films, and music were similarly censored. Music and lyrics by popular bands, such as New Kids on the Block, were seen as far too risqué for the young and impressionable Hudson children. Instead, they would listen to the likes of the soundtrack from the film *Sister Act* or suitable gospel songs, such as "Amazing Grace."

☙ *Katy Perry, global superstar.*

Such spiritual sensibilities are a far cry from the successful, sexy artist we're familiar with today. However, Katy's inimitable style and versatility in fashion choices—which range from pop princess to 1950s siren to sultry sexpot—can be traced back to her early days in Santa Barbara. At the age of nine, Katy started taking lessons in dance, including a number of swing steps such as the Lindy Hop or jitterbug. This gave her a love of some of the incredible styles women wore during the 1950s.

Learning to dance wasn't enough for Katy—she was unable to hide her desire to perform and she wanted the spotlight for more than just dancing. When Angela was eleven, nine-year-old Katy would watch her leave for singing lessons. Later, when Angela came home after class she would practice her songs and record herself rehearsing. It wasn't long before Katy started copying her. She would sneak into Angela's room and start taping herself secretly.

As Katy rehearsed the songs over and over, she began to show the tapes to her parents and perform for her family, dancing around the living room. Her talent was immediately obvious, and her parents realized they should do something to nurture it. So the Hudsons decided that, like her big sister, Katy could have singing lessons, too.

In a bid to get attention, Katy would sing anywhere, whether it was for a rapt congregation in a church hall or for smitten coffee drinkers in a crowded café. Katy loved being in the spotlight and thrived on it—perhaps as the result of being a middle child. Whoever her audience was, when Katy sang, people sat up and took notice.

 hard worker, even as a teenager, Katy was keen to learn her trade as a singer and musician. She even superglued the tips of her fingers once because they hurt so much from practicing her guitar all day. Yet her rebellious side was slowly emerging, especially when she decided to pierce her own nose.

Despite this, her parents continued to be supportive. When she was only fifteen, her mother took her on several trips to Nashville, where she recorded an album entitled *Katy Hudson* (2001), which consisted of gospel rock songs. Sadly, the label went under, and the album only sold 200 copies. But none of this deterred Katy from forging on.

Dropping the name Hudson and taking her mother's maiden name of Perry, Katy moved to Los Angeles when she was seventeen, filled with hope about her career as a successful recording artist. She was taken under the wing of one of America's foremost producers, Glen Ballard, who helped Katy develop her talent. It was an exciting time for the young singer—she was on the verge of having all her dreams come true. There she was, in Hollywood and with the world at her feet.

ut only two years later, at nineteen, Katy was broke and on the brink of giving up all hope. She had been dropped by numerous record labels and no one wanted to take on yet another solo female artist.

Katy's metamorphosis into one of the twenty-first century's leading pop icons is a journey of belief, perseverance, and talent. Thanks to the support of her fans, including stars such as Madonna—a self-declared fan—Katy has become a music sensation. Today, she has sold more than 37,620,000 million digital tracks in the United States alone, as well as more than 11 million albums world-wide, which makes her one of the best-selling artists of all time.

As one of the world's leading pop artists, Katy has also been a part of several high-profile entertainment ventures. In the United Kingdom, she was a guest judge on the seventh season of the British television show *The X Factor* and was also called upon to perform on the ninth season of *American Idol*. In 2011, Katy was the voice of Smurfette in the animated feature film *The Smurfs*, alongside costars Neil Patrick Harris, Hank Azaria, and Sofía Vergara.

Katy Perry has also been building her brand. In November 2010 she released a perfume known as *Purr*, which became the best-selling fragrance during the first nine weeks of its release. In December 2011, she released another perfume *Meow*, which sold out in pre-orders before it was even available. Along with her award-winning, chart-topping music career, Katy Perry has also become a successful, dynamic businesswoman. A star across the globe, this is her story.

1

BEING

Katy Hudson

efore Katy Perry evolved into the sexy, raven-haired, "Katy Perry: Pop Icon," she was Kathryn Hudson—a naïve, flaxen-haired daughter of two Christian pastors—who spent her early childhood traveling around the country with her parents.

Born in Santa Barbara on October 25, 1984 Katy and her brother and sister enjoyed an interesting childhood. From the ages of three to eleven, they moved with their parents from town to town founding churches. With no fixed home, at various times the family lived in Oklahoma, Arizona, and Florida.

Just as Katy made new friends in a new place, her family would move on to the next location. It seems that learning to adapt to new situations made her outgoing, outspoken, and vibrant from an early age.

Her childhood was hardly the rock and roll lifestyle she lives today. Katy remembers at the age of eight going antique hunting with her father early on Saturday mornings, or "going to garage sales or the house of someone who'd recently passed away whose family were selling everything."

By the time Katy was eleven, her parents had set up a more permanent home in Santa Barbara—an idyllic setting for any child in the 1990s. The beach town, sometimes referred to as the American Riviera, lies on the south California coast and is a mecca for tourists across America.

Keith and Mary settled into life in the Southern California town, living a God-fearing life and preaching. However, it hadn't always been that way. Both of them had had their fair share of fun and adventure before they found each other and turned their lives around.

Keith (born Maurice Keith Hudson in June 1947) was raised in Memphis, and became part of the Strawberry Fields Forever group in the 1960s, a group of people who were behind the campaign for Timothy Leary to be elected governor

of California. A controversial figure in the 1960s and 1970s, Leary was an icon for recreational drug users as he advocated psychedelic drug research and promoted the spiritual benefits of LSD.

If that weren't enough of a rock and roll pedigree, Keith played the tambourine on stage for Sly and the Family Stone, a famous American rock, funk, and soul band based out of California. The band was seen as pioneers of soul, funk, and psychedelic music.

"Dad would have died from one tab too many," Katy said in an interview with the *Daily Telegraph.* "They both had a wild life, then they found God and felt like they needed to have a personal change—that's how they decided to raise me." Katy's father Keith now runs the Keith Hudson Ministries.

Katy's mother, Mary, has also had a colorful past. Born Mary Christine Perry in December 1947, she came from a wealthy California family. Her father Frank J. Perry was a stockbroker, and her mother was Pauline Schwab, whose brother Charles M. Schwab founded the Bethlehem Steel Corporation.

Katy has claimed that her mother Mary went on a date with rock legend Jimi Hendrix back in the 1960s. "He just came up to her in a club and picked her out," Katy said. Mary then went on to marry an English race-car driver and farm macadamia nuts in Zimbabwe before becoming a radio reporter with ABC, for whom she interviewed Muhammad Ali and President Jimmy Carter among others.

All of this is a far cry from the devout, God-fearing Christian lives the couple built for their three children Angela, Katy, and David.

Above: A yearbook picture of the young Katy, showing her naturally lighter-colored hair.

Opposite: The Katy Perry known to her fans today.

By the book

Katy's parents met in the 1970s. Mary first saw Keith while she was reporting on a tent revival—a gathering of Christian worshippers in a tent used for revival meetings, church rallies, and healing crusades. They married and embraced the Christian faith as the core of their life as they were "born again." They tried to instill a solid Christian foundation in their children, and keep them safe from any of the harmful influences that they, themselves, had indulged in during the carefree days of the 1960s and 70s.

The Hudsons now minister throughout the United States and internationally, going to countries such as France, Belgium, Singapore, Malaysia, Italy, and Germany—working hard as Christian evangelists.

Though Katy's parents have become successful Christian preachers, with their own ministry, their daughter didn't have to look too far to find examples of success in the entertainment world, as members of her mother's family had carved out successful careers in Hollywood.

Mary's older brother Frank Perry and his wife Eleanor were successful in Hollywood as a director and screenwriter, respectively. Eleanor wrote a number of suspense novels, before working with her second husband, Frank Perry. They received an Oscar nomination for their joint project *David and Lisa*. There was no getting away from it: Katy had entertainers and talent in her bloodline and she wasn't going to ignore it. Growing up in the Hudson household, however, meant no "secular music" was played in the house, and the children spent a lot of their time reading or studying the Bible. It was God's way or no way. All the family radios in the house were tuned to Gospel radio stations.

Kathryn Hudson and her siblings Angela (two years older) and brother David (four years younger) were brought up to be protected from the outside world. Pop music and other secular influences were all banned from the house.

As a result, the children spent their time at Christian schools and Christian camps with visits to church several times a week. One of the schools Katy and her siblings went to was the Santa Barbara Christian School, an elementary school tucked in the shadow of the Emmanuel Lutheran Church in Santa Barbara. It was a simple life and a protected one, where the children followed a specific and controlled Christian path. In fact, Katy has since said: "I didn't have a childhood. I come from a very non-accepting family, but I'm very accepting."

When Katy was nine members of her parents' church were beginning to recognize her vocal talents. She was a member of the choir and would belt out gospel songs such as "His Eye is on the Sparrow," "Amazing Grace" (all eight verses), or "Oh Happy Day" for members of the congregation.

Katy found her own ways of getting around her parents' strict rules. When they weren't looking, she would get her friends to sneak CDs into the house. Once Katy had the CDs, she would use a down comforter to cover the cracks under her bedroom door, which muffled the sounds of the tunes she wanted to listen to. Her siblings would do the same thing, listening to illicit music in their bedrooms with the volume down as low as it could go.

Katy's parents were so strict that even the word "Devil" was banned in the house: appetizers such as deviled eggs were renamed "angeled eggs," while even the popular household item—the miniature hoover known as the "Dirt Devil"—was forbidden to cross the Hudsons' threshold. Breakfast, too, could be a minefield; the cereal Lucky Charms, a popular morning treat for children across America, was not allowed. The brand contained the word "lucky" which, to Mary's evangelical ears, sounded like "Lucifer."

One night at a teenage slumber party, Katy was introduced to Queen—a band she had never heard before. This was like a spiritual awakening. She spent hours in her bedroom listening to the forbidden tunes and became a huge fan of Freddie Mercury, an artist who was the total antithesis of everything her parents believed in. To Katy, Queen and Freddie Mercury's musicality and lyrics were flamboyant and real. But, to her parents, listening to his type of music was akin to devil worship.

"Soul sister"

The Hudson children were desperate to be like other teens—watching VH1 or MTV, enjoying fun teen movies, and listening to the latest chart hits. They spent time with their friends after school enjoying forbidden TV shows. On these occasions, Angela and Katy would get to watch films such as *Dirty Dancing* over and over again.

Though the siblings were close, Katy was the middle child and, like many middle children, she fought for attention from her parents and often managed to command it, too. Her natural talent for music meant

> Wow *this is ammo. I'm able to say what I think and put it on a bed of music. It made me feel magical.*

that when she sang, no one could miss her. Her siblings loved to hear her sing and called her "Katy Bird" as she sang them to sleep. It wasn't long before her parents started paying attention to her talents. Katy Perry's future as a pop star was honed from a young age—the dance moves, the choreography, the onstage confidence—all thanks to some healthy sibling rivalry back in the family home in Santa Barbara.

When Katy was nine, her elder sister Angela was having singing lessons. Katy, who had begun to realize she had a passion for music, desperately wanted to join in. Every day, she heard her eleven-year-old sister singing Christian songs through the walls of her bedroom as Angela practiced over and over again, singing into

cassettes and learning the tunes. After a while, Katy couldn't stop herself. Like younger sisters the world over, she just had to copy her sister. She had to do everything Angela did. And it wasn't just about "borrowing" her sister's clothes or playing with her toys. Katy would sneak into Angela's bedroom and take the tapes back into her own bedroom.

"I picked up a Carman track . . . 'River of Life' by Carman," Katy said in an interview with *Christian Music Central*. "I copied every little thing she did. It was actually her tape, but I stole it. So I took it and I practiced it and I performed it before she did."

Once she had learned the songs Katy began to take them to her parents and get them to listen. Instantly recognizing their daughter's talent, they decided that even though Katy was only nine, she should start having singing lessons, too. From that time she began to sing gospel and Christian songs, learning every note and making sure she was pitch perfect.

Realizing how special their daughter's voice was, her parents encouraged her to sing in church. Katy couldn't wait to sing in front of an audience. She would eagerly head off to church, stand before the congregation, and sing. Her confidence was incredible, as her family watched on with pride. It was here that Katy got an appetite for attention. When she sang in the church, she loved everyone looking at her. "Everyone would drop what they were doing and all eyes would be on me," said Katy. "I felt really powerful."

She would also get up and sing in coffeehouses, farmers' markets, restaurants, and any crowded venue. "Wherever I went, restaurants or whatever, I would get up and sing 'Amazing Grace,'" Katy said. The world became her stage, and crowds were an opportunity to entertain.

At the age of nine, Katy began to take dance classes at a recreation building in Santa Barbara. By the time she was thirteen, she got her hands on a guitar. It was the gateway for the young Katy to a whole new world of music. "It was like, wow, this is ammo. I'm able to say what I think and put it on a bed of music. It made me feel magical," said Katy.

As she continued to sing at their church, Katy's parents began to realize that there could be a larger audience ready to hear their talented daughter sing.

GOSPEL MUSIC

Though Katy Perry is now known as a pop icon, people tend to forget that she started out as a gospel singer. Gospel had a huge influence on the young Katy.

Had things worked out differently, she could have been a gospel star, rather than a global pop artist. Gospel was one of the few genres of music that Katy's parents allowed in the house when their children were growing up. Katy would sing gospel tracks at home and at church—it became a big part of her early life.

African American gospel music, based on American folk music, is marked by strong rhythms and elaborate refrains, incorporating elements of spirituals, blues, and jazz. One such artist, Yolanda Adams, is a Grammy-award-winning, multi-million-selling artist who is known as the First Lady of Gospel. Powerful and successful gospel artists such as Adams and CeCe Winans through to The Canton Spirituals and Virtue were all popular recording artists when Katy was a teenager.

These artists, in turn, had been themselves influenced by gospel legends such as James Cleveland or the Edwin Hawkins Singers, and by jazz icons Nancy Wilson and Stevie Wonder. Another key influence on Katy's career was Mahalia Jackson—known as "The Queen of Gospel"—who recorded about thirty albums (mostly for one of Katy's future record labels, Columbia) during her career. A mentor to the likes of Aretha Franklin and Della Reese, Jackson's 45-rpm records included a dozen million-sellers.

Growing up with these strong influences helped Katy understand music. Although many people now think of Katy as purely a pop artist, her ability to write catchy songs comes of her lengthy education in gospel music. She spent many years studying different schools of music, but started writing songs for the Christian music market at as young an age as thirteen.

Along with gospel, Katy was also exposed to Contemporary Christian Music. Known as CCM or "inspirational music," this genre of popular music covers the Nashville, Tennessee–based rock and pop Christian music legacy, whose representatives include Avalon, BarlowGirl, Jeremy Camp, Casting Crowns, Steven Curtis Chapman, David Crowder Band, Amy Grant, Natalie Grant, Jars of Clay, MercyMe, Newsboys, Michael W. Smith, Rebecca St. James, Third Day, and TobyMac, among others. Katy, too, was briefly a part of this movement when she moved to Nashville and began writing and recording her first album.

After Katy left Nashville for L.A., record companies had some trouble reconciling the image of the former gospel singer with that of a burgeoning pop artist. However, Katy wasn't the first artist to make this crossover into the mainstream.

Marie Osmond, who has a passing resemblance to Katy, was also raised within a strong Christian faith and, by the time she was a teenager, was a teen idol and a pinup across America, while never losing sight of her religious beliefs.

Other artists, such as Sam Cooke, have also managed to cross over from gospel to more mainstream pop music. Like Katy, Cooke was the son of a preacher and began his career singing in a gospel group with his brothers and sisters before moving on to other groups and recording a huge number of gospel songs. And like Katy, Cooke too had changed his name; while she went from Katy Hudson to Katy Perry, Cooke—not wishing to alienate his gospel fans—recorded a pop single under the name Dale Cook. However, his sound was so distinctive, his alias didn't stick and, pretty soon, Sam Cooke was a recognized and incredibly successful R&B artist with top-40 hits in the pop charts and the R&B charts. Just like Katy.

Gospel propelled Katy into the music world and, despite her present-day style, it remains at her core—helping her be the artist she is today.

GOSPEL SINGERS SUCH AS YOLANDA ADAMS WERE A HUGE INFLUENCE ON THE YOUNG KATY ☞

"I've tried to stay as **TRUE TO**

MYSELF as possible and I think

that's what really **RESONATES**  with

the **CONNECTION** with people that

admire my **MUSIC** . They **SEE**

that. I think that I will not **WIN** in any

way **SHAPE OR FORM** if I do things

out of wrong motives or if they're not

ORGANIC . I'm **MATURING** as a

person, but I'm still as **CUCKOO**

and **CRAZY**  as I've always been."

Nashville Bound

By the age of fifteen, Katy's career was on an upward trajectory. Singing as Katy Hudson, she was gaining attention as a gospel singer and a Christian artist. For an artist like her, the best place to go was Nashville, Tennessee—center of the world's Christian music scene. Katy had attracted the attention of a few rock veterans from Nashville, who wanted her to come to the Christian music heartland, Tennessee, to polish her writing skills. She and her mother started to make regular trips to Music City.

Music Row, southwest of downtown Nashville, houses the Christian pop and rock music industries. Over in the heart of Nashville, there are hundreds of businesses related to contemporary Christian music industries. Far from Santa Barbara, Katy was transported to a mass of low-rise, suburban-looking, concrete offices, filled with music executives from record labels, publishing houses, music licensing firms, recording studios, video production houses, and other businesses all linked with the music industry.

"It seemed like everybody knew everybody else and I didn't know anyone," Katy later told *Christian Music Central*. "It made me feel like the new kid all over again, just like growing up."

Katy and her mother would stay at the AmeriSuites in Franklin, just south of Nashville near the Interstate 65. While there, she and her mother met a number of record producers and writers. Katy was signed by Red Hill Records, an independent Christian record label. Red Hill was established in 2000 as a sub label of Pamplin Music, one of the top five Christian music record labels then. It looked like Katy Hudson had made it. Still only fifteen, she had been signed on by a record label. But as she swiftly learned, getting a contract from a label doesn't necessarily guarantee success.

Naturally, Katy was going to make the most of her opportunity. A prolific songwriter, she wrote or co-wrote a number of songs for her album. On March 6, 2001, she

"Last Call," "Growing Pains," "Naturally," "My Own Monster" & "When There's Nothing Left" produced by David Browning for the Levi-Howard Music Group Engineered by Paul Jenkins & David Browning

"Trust in Me," "Spit" and "Faith Won't Fail" produced by Otto Price for Juggernaut Entertainment. Engineered by Paul Jenkins & Otto Price

"Search Me" & "Piercing" produced by Tommy Collier for Gymnotic Productions Engineered by Paul Jenkins Tommy Collier

katy hudson.

released her first single, "Trust In Me." This was followed by the release of her album on October 23, 2001—two days before her seventeenth birthday. Her family hoped this gospel album, entitled *Katy Hudson*, would be her ticket to fame and fortune.

The album received a number of positive reviews. Russ Breimeier, reviewing her album for *Christianity Today*, commented: "Katy Hudson's debut easily could have been just another teen songwriter mimicking mainstream music trends with Christian lyrics. Instead, I hear a remarkable young talent emerging, a gifted songwriter in her own right who will almost certainly go far in this business. That name again is Katy Hudson. Trust me, you'll be hearing it more and more in the next year."

Despite such acclaim, the album only sold around two hundred copies, reaching 198 in the Allmusic Christian Charts. The dream finally came to an end as Red Hill Records, her label, went into liquidation. The company was bankrupt.

According to Katy:

"When I made my gospel record, I was fifteen, and I was still kinda under my parent's household, and beyond that, that was the only thing that really mattered to me at that moment as a fifteen-year-old young lady. And so, I sang about that, and that was the only thing I knew. I didn't really have any other social life, or I didn't know pop culture because growing up, I grew up with two ministers as parents, two parents as ministers and so everything was really related to faith. So naturally, I sang about what I knew, which was that. And then, I had a very short-lived career, if you would even call it a career, maybe a couple-month career in the gospel music industry that didn't last long. I wanted to be successful, but unfortunately, my record label that signed me, they went under and so did my record."

Katy decided it was time for a change. She had an opportunity to move to L.A. and, to avoid any confusion with the Hollywood actress Kate Hudson, Katy adopted her mother's maiden name "Perry." As Katy Perry, she took another step on the journey from Gospel singer to Rock star.

The cover art and CD insert for Katy's first album, recorded under the name Katy Hudson.

Katy would like to thank:
Todd Randall: you are one out of many who have through this industry and continues to open doors glad we can chill as friends all the time rather than kids. That is so special to me. Anna-Banana: Oh m can't believe how you bust your chops for me. Th process you have given 100% encouragement....I already. Only the best producers: David - Brotha. rocked. You gave me my first Beatles record. (luv Thanks. Otto: How many times can I say I love you .....well besides all the B.E.T. 24/7. Tommy: thanks fo what vibe is all about. You have a sweet heart (be catfish). Me and mom will always keep you in our Jenkins: thanks for adding your special raw.....not completely Nashville sound to the mix. Luv yah. Brian Whit Marino: Thanks for taking a chance. Serious. You're like a mentor. You inspire me. Serious. You're like a mentor. taking me under your wings even when it w job. A heart of gold. Pamplin Pub: You go me grounded (literally) I love your suppo Cyka, Mark Classen and Dan Michaels friends not forgotten. I miss your crazy is your record too. Beth Blinn: You ha me the ways. You are the sweetest around here. Melissa Hambrick - t all your help! Elissa V: Thanks for s me how to develop as me in th timing. I understand now. Joey CREW!) Your efforts won't go ur warded... believe me. Kristen B being your sassifrass. You actuall made this chick look o.k.!

Dad, Mom, Tang, Dav (grandma): being my Katy-Bird. You really don't know how much I love you guys. (Mom Thanks for developing me and my character. There is no price I could pay for that. S.B. crew, Dream Center. My church Oasis: I represent. Eve: I love being your best friend. My inspirers: Mark and Martha.... Agath Danoff... You have so much wisdom in this area...thank you for sharing it, Bob Pamplin & Gary Randall: Thank you so much for taking a chance on this little girl. My Lord: remember the gift You gave me? The one with music and affecting peoples' lives through it. Well here it is. I'm giving it back to You....through my life....through my music..through souls for the kin heaven. I love You. You kno

BECOMING
Katy Perry

**A**fter the failure of her album and the bankruptcy of her record label, Katy returned home devastated. She needed a plan. She wasn't going to give up, but her options were limited.

Up to that point, Katy had been best known as a Christian artist and a gospel singer. One of her producers in Nashville had suggested that Katy rethink her sound but, having had such a sheltered childhood, she didn't have a wide diversity of influences or references. She had no idea who she would want to work with or what to do next. The answer came to her one night when she was in a hotel room in Nashville.

Katy was watching VH1, a channel that was usually banned in the Hudson household, and saw producer Glen Ballard talking about Alanis Morissette. It was a "lightbulb" moment for Katy—she really felt he was someone she could work with.

Using the connections she had made during her time in Nashville, Katy sought out anyone who knew the esteemed music producer. At last, one of her contacts was able to get her a meeting with Glen, which turned out to be a life-changing encounter.

On the day of her audition with the legendary producer, Katy was so terrified that she wouldn't make the grade that she made her father wait in the car for her. "I said, 'Dad, stay in the car . . . I'm just gonna go in, play a song for this guy and come back out.' And I did, and I guess it went well, because I got the call the next day."

Katy's audition went so well, in fact, that she was invited to relocate and join Glen in Los Angeles. It was a fantastic opportunity for her. Still, she was only seventeen, and there was one snag—Katy's parents insisted that she graduate high school before making the move Los Angeles.

Determined to succeed, Katy buckled down to take the GED (General Educational Development test) in order to get the equivalent of a high school diploma. In the end, she passed with flying colors and was able to focus once again on her career. She spent hours listening to Glen's songs, learning his music, and absorbing his style. Glen, in turn, reassured Katy's parents that she would be taken care of. He, as her mentor, was going to keep an eye on her.

With a new car, some new music, and revived dreams, Katy set off to Los Angeles—like so many other dreamers had done before her—to make her fortune. When she'd traveled before, she had usually had chaperones or parents nearby. Now she was on her own in a new city, which proved to be quite different from her former sheltered lifestyle.

"When I started out in gospel music," she said, "my perspective then was a bit enclosed and very strict, and everything I had in my life at that time was church-related. . . . So when I left home and saw all of that [L.A.], it was like, 'Omigosh, I fell down the rabbit hole and there's this whole Alice in Wonderland right there!'"

Katy was friends with Matt Thiessen, the lead singer of Christian rock band Relient K. By 2001, Relient K had released *The Anatomy of the Tongue in Cheek*, which put them in the Christian rock limelight. Matt continued to collaborate with Katy, who was still working out who she was and what kind of direction her music should take.

It wasn't just Katy's music that was on the verge of change, however. When Katy was part of the Nashville music scene, she had failed to create a distinct style. She would sing in front of audiences wearing baggy jeans, sneakers and flip-flops as well as bandana-style headbands. This wasn't going to work in Los Angeles. Katy had a lot of work in front of her. Not only did she have to develop an onstage persona, but she also had to define her voice as an artist.

Katy onstage at the 2011 American Music Awards, L.A., November 20, 2011.

ALANIS MORISSETTE

On June 13, 1995, Alanis Morissette's album *Jagged Little Pill* was released in the U.S. No one could have predicted the album's popularity, or just how many artists would be influenced by the Canadian's songs.

A former child star, Morissette had moved from her native Canada to L.A. to work with Glen Ballard, one of America's foremost music producers, on her first internationally released album. Their collaboration on *Jagged Little Pill* spawned six hit singles, including the worldwide smash "Ironic," which was nominated for a Grammy. The album went platinum in the U.S. (sixteen times) and sold over 30 million copies. The emotional theme of the songs and their powerful lyrics affected the next wave of female artists, such as Shakira and Pink, and the album remains influential today.

As Morissette was making a name for herself across the globe, Katy Perry was just starting her singing lessons in her hometown of Santa Barbara—their worlds couldn't have been further apart.

For someone like Katy, whose strict parental restrictions resulted in a limited knowledge of pop music, it was not easy to discover different artists. Katy had lived a sheltered life, only managing to listen to the odd Queen record, or anything else her friends smuggled through to her. Morissette's work happened to be one of those, as Katy remembered: "And then there was Alanis Morissette. *Jagged Little Pill* was huge for me. One of the vivid memories of my childhood is swinging on the swing set singing 'Ironic' at the top of my lungs. I went to Christian school, so I got into a little trouble for that one."

Years later, when trying to develop a new sound in Nashville, Katy gradually came to realize that life as a gospel artist wasn't working out for her—with her first album selling only two hundred copies and her record label going under, her choices were limited. However, there were other producers who still believed in her and one of her contacts in Nashville

asked her whom she'd like to work with to further her career. She had no idea.

Katy went back to her hotel room in Nashville, and tuned into a station usually banned in her home: "I turned on VH1 and saw Glen Ballard talking about Alanis Morissette," said Katy. "I thought, 'You know what? I want to work with him!'"

After Katy had decided that Ballard was the man for her, a meeting was set up between the pair and Katy went to audition for him. She won him over and was invited to move to Los Angeles to get to work on some new songs with her idol's mentor.

In 2003, Ballard gave an interview to *Off the Radar* about his new artist who, at this stage, was still known as Katy Hudson: "I'm not going to take my artist Katy Hudson and say 'You gotta be a rap artist now because I think it would be really cool.' I think putting the round peg in the square hole, it will never work. My thing is really starting with the artist. If it happens to be a little bit out of vogue at that point, I really don't care."

Glen was asked: "You mentioned your artist Katy Hudson, is that Kate Hudson, the actress?" He replied: "No, I don't think anyone will confuse Kate Hudson for Katy Hudson once this record is out."

When talking about Katy's music, Glen compared her to his former charge, Alanis, saying: "It's in the Alanis Morissette singer/songwriter female, that's the box you can put her in but I don't think she'll stay in that box long. She's such a huge star and a great singer and a complete person. We don't put out many new records so I really want this to be great. I'm mostly working on other stuff, but this one's a winner."

As Katy has matured as an artist, she continues to express her admiration for Alanis. In fact, in 2010, Katy said: "I feel like you're missing an Alanis Morissette in 2010. I love how she was a voice for a lot of people who couldn't explain their feelings"—a skill that Katy has been honing since she burst onto the scene.

KATY HAS ACKNOWLEDGED THE EFFECT THAT THE MUSIC OF ALANIS MORISSETTE HAD ON HER DURING HER TEENAGE YEARS.

Katy started experimenting with a diverse group of artists during her formative years in Los Angeles. Alongside Glen Ballard, Katy wrote a track with Mickey Avalon, an American rapper from Hollywood with a highly controversial reputation. Although the rapper was also raised in a religious home (Orthodox Jewish), his background was far from wholesome, his songs reflecting his experiences with substance abuse and prostitution. Mickey seemed to have nothing in common with Katy, but they both shared a love of music and a desire to write and perform. Katy had fun with Mickey. He represented her new life in Los Angeles, which meant freedom of expression and a break from the former constraints of her religious background.

Together with Mickey, Katy wrote the song "Highs with the Lows" [aka "High and the Lows"]. The song quickly died away, receiving one airplay (due to its controversial lyrics) when Mickey Avalon was a guest on the radio show *Loveline* on KROQ.

Lines such as "*Preacher McGrath was always eager to ask . . . Why his mother rubbed her hands beneath his pants at mass*" or "*Her papa was a preacher so she knew the good book . . . And when he tucked her into bed, he fondled the nook*" were typical for an artist like Mickey, but a total departure for someone like Katy, whose previous work had usually celebrated her Christian faith or God.

Though it's generally thought that Katy cowrote the track, she was never officially registered as a cowriter on "Highs with the Lows" with the American Society of Composers, Authors, and Publishers (ASCAP). The song has slowly faded into obscurity.

Another artist Katy collaborated with was Printz Board. Katy had already known him through a mutual friend when they started working on the track "Rock God." Unlike her collaboration with Mickey, "Rock God" was a song for the album Katy was working on with Glen. Printz is an acclaimed producer, writer, and artist who, alongside

Will.i.am, shaped The Black Eyed Peas, and has worked with artists such as Macy Gray, John Legend, and Busta Rhymes. Katy was working with the best. Printz and Katy spent hours in the recording booth, working and enjoying each other's company as they finished the track together.

One of Katy's most consistent cowriters during this period, apart from Glen, was her then boyfriend, musician Matt Thiessen. Together with Glen, the pair wrote her track "The Box." The lyrics seemed to capture the journey Katy was on: *"I started living outside of the box . . . Crossing over lines where I always used to stop."* Living in Los Angeles meant meeting people from different cultural backgrounds, musical genres, and lifestyles. As a result, Katy was distancing herself more and more from her parents' beliefs and way of life.

Katy continued to work hard. She spent months working with Glen, and together they wrote songs such as "Weigh Me Down," "Oh Love Let Me Sleep," "LA Don't Take It Away," "The Better Half of Me," "Simple," "Longshot" (which features a video of her gazing romantically at Matt Thiessen), and "Sherlock Holmes." Katy was signed by Island Def Jam records. The album was due for release in 2005, so they had a few years of work ahead of them. Once again, it

looked like Katy was on her way to breaking through as a recording artist.

The label, Island Def Jam records, had been formed in 1999, when Universal Music Group—one of the world's biggest recording companies—merged two of its companies, Island Records and Def Jam Recordings.

Katy continued to work on the project and was excited about the new album, which would be her follow-up to *Katy Hudson*. In 2003, however, Katy was dropped by Island Def Jam Records, leaving her devastated. She had gotten so close to completing and releasing another album—with a whole new sound—and it looked like all her hard work had been in vain.

Despite the fact that Katy was working with some of the country's leading writers and producers, it wasn't enough for Island Def Jam. Her image was proving a problem. Who was she? What was she? She had a "pop" air about her, but, despite the nature of her new songs, everyone knew that she had come from a gospel background. The label wasn't sure what to do with her or how to market her.

No one denied that Katy had talent, but, at this stage, she was just another young, feisty, and talented pop artist living in Los Angeles with big dreams.

"For me, it's really easy for me to write about heartache, really easy. I don't know why. I think that's how I get through it is by writing about the heartache that I'm having about a relationship, or a boy, or you know, someone I was in love with or hurt by or whatever."

THE NEXT BIG THING!

Katy Perry

This pastor's daughter says she has done bad things. What kind of things?

BY NICK DURDEN
PHOTOGRAPHY BY JUSTIN STEPHENS

"I'M COMPLETELY OUTRAGEOUS and I'll do anything for attention!" No, not the words of Paris Hilton, but the claim of a pastor's daughter.

"Music wasn't allowed in the house because it's the devil's work," says Katy Perry, a vocalist with the production team The Matrix. "And if I brought home friends, my mom wanted to know if they were Christians." Here, she laughs wildly as if someone, somewhere, just cracked a joke. "That's my parents. They're crazy! They're nuts!"

Perry, now 19, was born in Santa Barbara, and like Beyoncé, got her first taste of performance singing in church. Unlike Beyoncé, she spent her adolescence not being "your typical Christian," she says with a wicked laugh. "I've done a lot of bad things. Use your imagination."

After years singing locally, she came to the attention of The Matrix — the brain trust behind Avril Lavigne and Ricky Martin — who were assembling a group that now features Perry and British-born AKA. Their debut is a radio-friendly pop collection with Perry cast as a sunnier Avril.

"At first, I thought, 'Crap! There goes my credibility!' They've worked with some brilliant people, but also people who are hardly artists at all," she says. "But if people buy the record, that's all the credibility I need."

She's working on her solo debut (due 2005) with Morissette producer Glen Ballard. "My album will be more rock, which is probably why my parents think I'm going to hell!"

A total unknown working with the biggest names, Perry must have talent to burn. "No, I've just got really big boobs," she says. "And my sweater gets tighter every week. . . ." [BLENDER]

>>> OUT NOW **THE MATRIX** COLUMBIA

POP SONGS WITH PERRY CAST AS A SUNNIER AVRIL.

DRESS FROM **SLOW** ON MELROSE

Next big thing?

Since Katy was now without a label, Glen decided to shelve the album for a while as they worked out what to do next. Katy was left pounding the streets of Los Angeles, going to auditions looking for any break she could find.

One such meeting was with the recording group The Matrix, who were looking for new male and female singers. The Matrix were hit-makers—during the early 2000s they had written and produced a series of hits for some high-profile artists. The three members of The Matrix were Scott Spock, Lauren Christy, and Graham Edward, and they had made their name writing and/or producing hits for the likes of Shakira ("Don't Bother"), Avril Lavigne ("Sk8er Boi" and "Complicated"), and Jason Mraz ("The Remedy [I Won't Worry]"). Now they wanted to work with Katy Perry.

After months of auditions, Katy and her male counterpart, an unknown British artist named Adam Longlands, were the lucky duo chosen to work with The Matrix. The hitmakers had an incredible track record. Avril Lavigne—who, just like Katy, had been dropped by her label—worked with The Matrix and went on to sell 12 million copies of her debut album. Furthermore, Avril, like Katy, had started off singing in church before gaining fame as a punk rock star. Katy's expectations were high.

Katy and Adam spent months recording tracks with The Matrix, and it looked like 2004 was going to be Katy's year. Bouncing back from the disappointment of Red Hill and Island Def Jam Records, Katy signed a deal with Columbia Records—which was interested in her album with Glen Ballard. With Columbia and The Matrix behind her, Katy's career looked to be back on track.

Katy's career trajectory was also attracting the attention of the media. The influential American music magazine *Blender* interviewed her for its "The Next Big Thing" column. It was a huge honor for Katy, and, after the article's appearance, other people in the music industry began to take notice. Katy was certainly one to watch.

Katy, Adam, and The Matrix worked hard to lay down a number of tracks and shoot some music videos. They recorded an entire album and started their press interviews. But, with only weeks to go before the disc's planned release in 2004, it was abruptly called off without explanation. (The Matrix later released the album on iTunes on January 27, 2009.)

At this stage, all Katy had left was her Columbia Records deal. The company was still talking to Katy and Glen about producing her album, and Katy even recorded a promotional DVD of music videos to garner publicity. Videos were shot for "Diamonds," "Simple," "Long Shot," "Box," "A Cup of Coffee," and "It's Okay to Believe." These videos were never aired on television, but Katy fans can still watch them on YouTube.

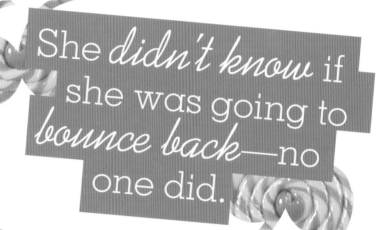

She *didn't know* if she was going to *bounce back*—no one did.

In order to test out Katy's popularity, Columbia Records released a limited-edition album that featured six of what the label felt were Katy's best songs. It was released on August 18, 2005, in Japan. Japan's failure to embrace Katy's music worried the record label, though, and soon afterward, Katy got the news she was dreading. In 2006, Columbia Records dumped Katy Perry.

According to Glen Ballard: "We tried so many labels. But, you know, it was the same with Alanis [Morissette]. Everybody turned her down. And then finally, Maverick puts *Jagged Little Pill* out and it's a huge hit. I think Katy was just maybe too ahead of her time."

Only in her early 20s, this was the third time that Katy had faced this kind of major professional disappointment. She didn't know if she was going to bounce back—no one did.

The article in *Blender* magazine that named Katy as the next big thing in 2004.

Keeping the faith

After having been dropped by Columbia Records, Katy was devastated. It looked like her roller-coaster career was over for good. Few people survive being dropped by two major record labels. Her sister, Angela, remembers Katy sitting on her bedroom floor, weeping. "I thought she wouldn't make it," said Angela. "She was heartbroken."

The trouble was, according to an executive at Columbia, that "Katy was too original." On a creative level, the company felt that they had done all they could and that Katy just wasn't going to work out. With two major failures behind her, the people around her were beginning to worry for her sanity, welfare, and career. The Columbia executive also noted: "You can get lost in L.A. She was going out, and she had the moment of realizing she was going in the wrong direction."

Los Angeles can be one long nonstop party town, and Katy was embracing it. She went out partying, making up for lost time. All of her hard work and years of sacrifice had left her broke and abandoned by the music industry, and her pride was crushed. She still hadn't tasted success, and it was proving hard for Katy to pick herself up.

"I had someone say to me that 'Psst, you should probably go home, because you're never gonna get signed again. You're pretty much damaged goods. And you should be in the defect aisle at Ross [clothing store chain],'" said Katy. "I'm like, 'I'm defected goods already?'" At the time, Katy was only twenty years old.

Despite her youth, Katy had written more than fifty songs with nearly every reputable songwriter in town. As she said in an interview later: "My Rolodex was filled with numbers to the brim, so why isn't this happening?" Katy decided to make a vow: If it didn't happen for her by the time she turned twenty-five, then she was going to refocus and rethink her career.

Even though the record label had dropped her, Katy still had one major supporter—Glen Ballard. He had spent so many years with Katy and refused to give up, staying by her side, even while Katy was acting out: "I encouraged Katy to not so much rebel against anything she's been through," said Glen, "but to actually use it toward defining who she really was as a person."

Katy began to pull herself out of her depression. She truly believed in her own ability, but being broke in Los Angeles was another struggle for the young singer. "I had the rug pulled out from under me so many times, and I didn't have any money," said Katy.

Unlike many other artists, Katy hadn't gotten a big advance from the record label. She was struggling financially, and her car— her beloved new Jetta— had been repossessed. Twice. Always the believer, though, Katy was writing checks and putting "Please God" on the memo line. Katy hadn't totally abandoned her Christian roots, but her faith was waning.

Katy was also keen to keep up appearances with her L.A. friends. No matter what. "I was just trying to live the life and trying to keep up with the Joneses," said Katy. "I wanted people to see me as someone they could really believe in."

She would go out to dinner with friends, order a salad, and hope her credit card wouldn't get declined at the end of the evening. These were tough times for Katy, as she survived on an unhealthy diet of potatoes, baked beans, Kraft singles, and an awful lot of Taco Bell.

Despite Katy's poverty and perceived lack of success, behind the scenes her music was slowly filtering into the world. Katy had a MySpace account, on which some of her collaborations with Glen Ballard were posted—tracks such as "Box," "Diamonds," and "Long Shot." Since her debut album had been shelved by Columbia, these songs were now floating around with no official home.

In June 2005, Katy got another break. Her song "Simple" was featured in the hit film *Sisterhood of the Traveling Pants*, based on the popular book by Ann Brashares. Katy's song was on the soundtrack, which was released by Columbia Records—her former record label—on May 24, 2005. It was something to celebrate, but, of course, Katy still had a few more hurdles to jump.

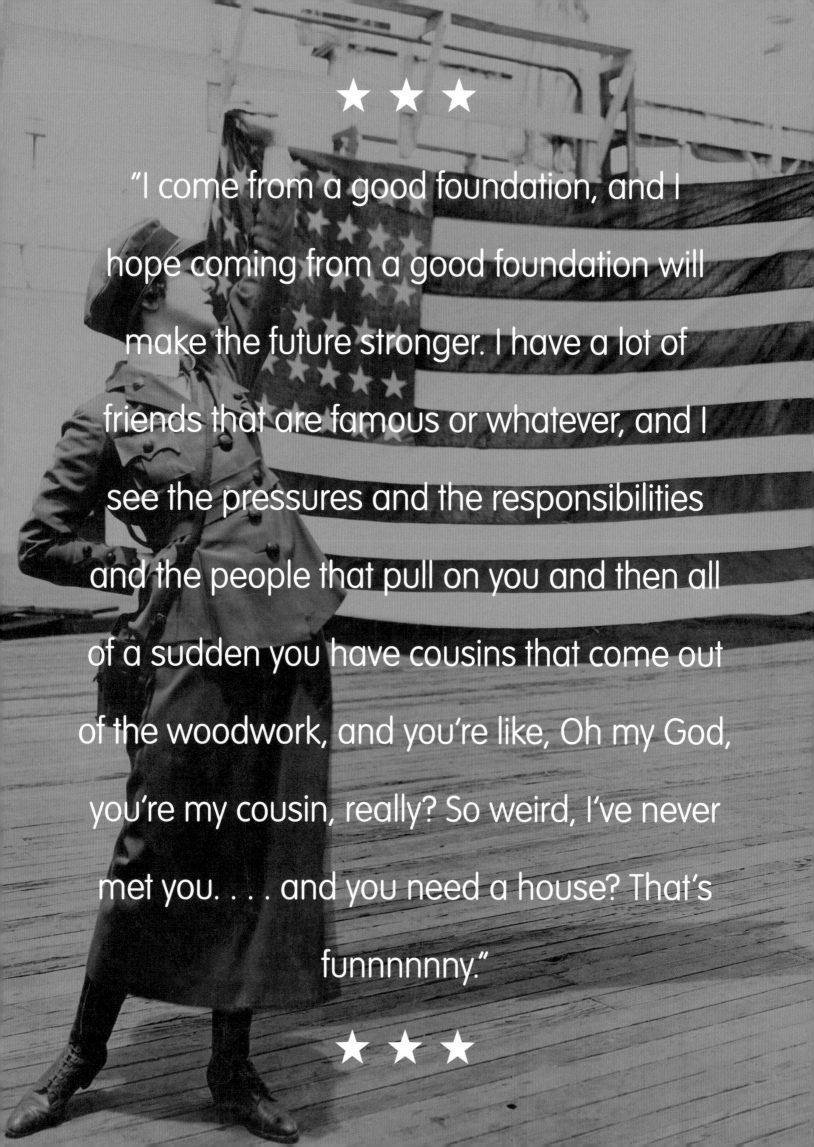

★ ★ ★

"I come from a good foundation, and I hope coming from a good foundation will make the future stronger. I have a lot of friends that are famous or whatever, and I see the pressures and the responsibilities and the people that pull on you and then all of a sudden you have cousins that come out of the woodwork, and you're like, Oh my God, you're my cousin, really? So weird, I've never met you. . . . and you need a house? That's funnnnnny."

★ ★ ★

Who's that girl?

Katy worked for a company that helped other artists get a break in the music industry before she got her own break.

Although one of her songs had appeared in a successful film, Katy was still chasing her dream and doing all she could to find work—ideally in her field as a singer—but nothing was happening for her. For years, the running joke between Katy and her family and friends had been "Are you famous yet?" Ready to grab any opportunities that came her way, Katy still had rent to pay, and bills were piling up. It was time to get a job.

So, in 2006, Katy joined TAXI, an A&R company based in the San Fernando Valley. TAXI, according to the company website, is "the world's leading Independent Artist & Repertoire Company. . . . Since 1992, TAXI has specialized in giving artists, bands, and songwriters real access to the people in the music business who have the power to sign deals. . . . Record companies, publishers, and music supervisors call us directly to find new artists and bands to sign. They also call to find hit songs, instrumentals and tracks for TV and film placements."

It was Katy's job to help fellow artists make it in the industry by introducing them to talent managers and producers, as well as dispensing advice. Katy hated it.

"That was the most depressing moment of my hustle," said Katy. "I was sitting there in a cubicle with twenty-five other trying-to-make-it-some-failed-artists in a box listening to the worst music you've ever heard in your entire life. Having no money, writing bad checks, renting a car after two cars had been repossessed, trying to give people constructive criticism and hope, when really I wanted to jump out of the building or cut my ears off and say, 'I can't help you! I can't catch a break. What am I gonna say to you? And you sing off tune.'"

Katy would spend hours in her "depressing" cubicle in the office at Calabasas, getting more and more frustrated. Time was passing, and she wasn't making inroads to fulfilling her dreams. The practicalities of life were getting in her way, but, despite that, she did her best to attend as many auditions as she could and refused to give up. Luckily, she still had Glen's support, and his contacts managed to get her some high-profile gigs.

The first of these gigs was with a band called Payable on Death—more commonly known as P.O.D.—a successful American Christian metal band that has sold more than 10 million records worldwide and earned three Grammy Award nominations. In 2006, Katy had the opportunity to work with them. It was only a small role, but it was something.

Katy provided backing vocals for the P.O.D. song "Goodbye For Now," and she also appeared in the video. Three minutes and twenty-seven seconds into the four-minute video, Katy appears next to the lead singer. It's a totally different Katy from the one we know today. Wearing fingerless gloves, a bandana around her neck, and a grungy vest over a white shirt, a dark-haired Katy belts out her lines. The current, colorful, sex bomb Katy Perry is nearly unrecognizable.

The song was a hit. It got a lot of radio play and was used in promotional videos for the film *The Chronicles of Narnia: The Lion, the Witch and the Wardrobe*. It also charted. The video, which featured Katy, reached the number-one spot on MTV's *Total Request Live* and became P.O.D.'s fourth number-one video.

In 2006, Carbon Leaf—a five-piece indie rock band from Richmond, Virginia, known for their alt-country, Celtic, and folk-infused sound—also featured Katy in a video for their song "Learn to Fly." Though Katy doesn't get to sing, she's the star of the video, racing across town to get to a Carbon Leaf gig.

Katy's next video appearance was alongside American rap rock band Gym Class Heroes. Again, she didn't get a chance to sing, but she played the eventual love interest of lead singer Travie McCoy in the song "Cupid's Chokehold."

"Cupid's Chokehold" climbed to number four on the Billboard Hot 100 and has sold nearly two million digital downloads, making it the band's highest-selling hit. It was another success for Katy, who had also made a significant impression on Travie. In fact, the pair ended up dating for a number of years. Meanwhile, after the video started appearing on television screens across America, people started asking, "Who's that girl?" Slowly, but surely, Katy was moving in the right direction again.

I KISSED A

Girl

In 2006, Katy was still working away in a job she hated with no good news in sight. She managed to book a few more gigs doing promotional work, but was totally unaware that her life was about to be turned completely around.

As Katy struggled with her life at TAXI, her name was being discussed among a number of executives at Capitol Records. The Capitol Music Group was a new record company formed by the merger of Capitol Records and Virgin Records and it was ready to sign new artists. If they signed Katy, it could be a case of third time's the charm for the California native. With a large number of songs written and waiting to go she just needed a label to get behind her.

There were three key people behind Katy's signing—Angelica Cob-Baehler, then a senior publicist at Capitol Records, executive Jason Flom, and his then junior representative Chris Anokute. All three were fans of Katy's work, despite the fact she had already been signed and dropped by two other major labels. Other executives might have seen Katy as damaged goods, but this trio felt that the talented singer-songwriter just hadn't been given a proper chance. She had talent—they just had to figure out how to market her.

Angelica was a huge fan of Katy Perry. Before working at Capitol Records, she had been a publicist at Columbia Records and knew that Katy had talent. According to Jeff Kempler, executive vice president of Virgin Records at the time Perry was signed, Chris Anokute was an "energetic cheerleader for the project and vocal proponent for Katy."

Jason Flom, meanwhile, had an impressive track record and was keen to bring Katy to Capitol Records. Jason is renowned in the industry for scouting talent. During his youth, as a young A&R executive, he broke new artists including Jewel, Hootie & the Blowfish, and Collective Soul. Jason then went on to found his own label, Lava Records. His artists sold more than 100 million records around the world by the time of its tenth anniversary. And now? He wanted Katy Perry.

In a letter Jason wrote to his friend, Bob Lefsetz—an American music industry figure and author of the e-mail newsletter and blog called the Lefsetz Letter—he wrote:

"Here's the real lowdown on Katy Perry: She was signed to (and dropped by) two major labels and in the process was put through the music business ringer. She spent several years working with many different producers only to find herself out on the street. Most people in her situation would have thrown in the towel but true stars persevere. . . . Around this time I hired Angelica Cob who had been a senior publicist at Katy's prior label. Angelica told me "You have to meet Katy Perry . . . she's a star." I got together with Katy at the Polo Lounge and she impressed me from the first moment with her charisma and her drive and then I heard her music and I was sold. I signed Katy on the basis of her voice and great songs that she had written. . . ."

Katy was at work when Jason called to confirm that, finally, she was being offered a new deal with a new company. It was something Katy never thought would happen.

In a later interview, Katy described the experience: "There were people that said, 'We've already spent money on her . . . We need fresh meat.' Everyone kind of looked at me a little bit like damaged goods, in a way. Like you see a soup can in an aisle in a grocery store and it's kind of, like, bent, you're not really going to buy that thing. Although the soup inside of it is probably still really delicious! There's, like, no difference. It's gonna be a great bowl of soup! . . . It took a wonderful group of people at Capitol to see beyond the dent and see that the dent was actually cool."

Opposite: Katy at the 2008 Vans Warped Tour kick-off party at the Key Club in West Hollywood.

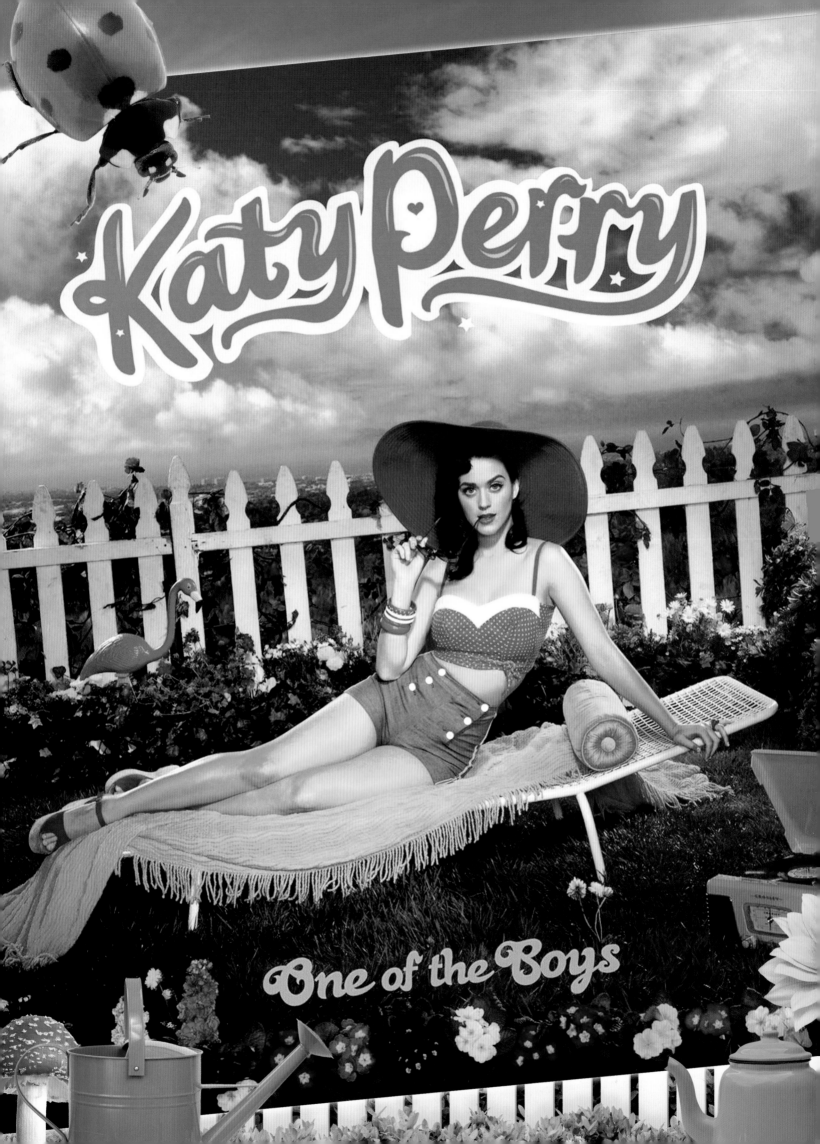

One of the boys

Now that Katy had finally been signed to a new record label, the hard work had to begin. Jason Flom still had to convince fellow executives at the Capitol Music Group that Katy was the breakthrough star they were looking for.

Jeff Kempler, the executive vice president of Virgin Records at the time of Perry's signing, remembers Jason's long-standing belief in Katy, which went back to the late summer of 2006.

A number of senior Virgin executives were on their way to visit the iTunes offices in Cupertino, and Jason used the travel time to tell the team all about Katy Perry, whom he believed could be their new global pop act. At the time, rumors were rife that Katy was about to be dropped by Columbia, and Jason wanted to play her tracks to his fellow execs on the car ride. "[Jason] proceeded to risk all of our hearing by playing us, at top volume, the records Katy had made for Columbia while he sang along to pretty much every line, especially 'Thinking of You' and 'Waking up in Vegas,'" remembers Jeff. Despite initial misgivings, Katy's music piqued their interest.

By the end of 2006, the execs at Virgin (soon to become the Capitol Music Group) were following Katy's journey. Though Columbia was letting her go, there were a few complications with her move. Since Katy was tied to Glenn, there was more red tape to sort through.

Katy's other major supporter, Angelica Cob-Baehler, insisted that Katy was worth investing in. She had worked with Katy at Columbia and felt that Jason and Jeff should negotiate a deal.

Jeff remembers: "At some point in or around January [2007], Jason told me he was dead set that we sign Katy. So in tandem with our head of business affairs, Phil Wild, we reopened direct conversations with Ballard and Katy's representatives and created a business structure that would facilitate Katy signing to Virgin, and bringing along her existing masters, with Columbia and Ballard's blessing." The masters were key, as they represented five years of hard work by Katy and Glen.

It was important for her new record company deal to get all of Katy's work, because, since she'd arrived in Los Angeles, she had written nearly seventy songs and had spent years honing a large number of them with some of the music industry's leading producers, writers, and musicians.

As Katy said in a later interview: "I've been working on my record since I was eighteen years old. I've gone through two record labels and written between sixty-five and seventy songs . . . It's been a long trip. I've had lots of money, lost lots of money, but the record's here and it's the right one."

After weeks of negotiating, the deal was finally signed—and included transfer of those vital masters. It was time to celebrate. Jeff recalls: "Jason had Katy come into a company-wide meeting to announce her signing, which Katy celebrated by blowing everyone away with an acoustic version of 'Thinking of You.'"

As it turned out, the song "Thinking of You" proved to be a hit with the execs. It ended up on her 2008 album One of the Boys and was the third song to be released as a single and was one of the tracks from the album written solely by Katy. Although the crowd that gathered at Capitol loved it, the record executives did have a few reservations.

According to Jeff Kempler, Jason felt that her Columbia recordings were very "strong but lacking an undeniable smash or two that would work both at U.S. pop radio and internationally." So, with the tracks now firmly in Capitol's hands, Jason's first action after Katy joined the company was setting up a collaboration between Katy and writer-producer Dr. Luke.

Katy shows off her new style on the cover of her first major album release, *One of the Boys*.

Looking for a hit

Now that Capitol Records had Katy on their list, they wanted to make sure that she delivered on her promise and potential. She needed a revamp and restyle both in the recording studio and out.

"Jason was very focused on supporting a collaboration between Katy and Dr. Luke in order to add to Katy's existing material," said Jeff Kempler, executive vice president at the company at the time. For, great

> You know . . . Me—Katy Perry—very *sassy*, cheeky, fun—cute, sexy and *smart*.

though Katy's material was, it still needed that ineffable something to ensure a few winners. "So, we were again wheeling and dealing to make that happen. The results are now well known: 'Hot & Cold' and 'I Kissed a Girl,' cowritten by Katy and Luke, were two of the biggest global hits of the decade."

Getting to that "global hit" stage was going to take months of hard work. Dr. Luke had cowritten and coproduced hit after hit, initially conquering the charts in 2004 after cowriting Kelly Clarkson's smash hit "Since U Been Gone," which reached number two on the *Billboard* Hot 100."

Dr. Luke frequently works with recording artists on turning their songs into huge worldwide smashes. Following his success with Kelly, he became the "go to" man of the moment, creating one worldwide megahit after another. "Apparently my taste is that of a thirteen-year-old girl," said Dr. Luke. "I'm trying to make songs that I love and make them feel a certain way and go to

certain places. It just so happens that a lot of thirteen-year-old girls like that."

Katy and Dr. Luke—a collaboration that would ultimately go on to spawn blockbusters—got to work in the studio. The pair had already met when she was at Columbia, but now it was time to turn Katy's tunes into bona fide hits for Capitol.

"Katy definitely knows what she wants and doesn't want," said Dr. Luke in a July 2010 interview with *Billboard*. "She has an amazing voice, great taste, and she makes great videos. It's nice to work with an artist who can deliver your music so well."

"There are all kinds of different shades [to the album]," Katy explained later in an interview. "Honestly, it's like a 'Dear diary,' and there are twelve chapters, and it's not just about one thing. And the thing of it is—I hope that people will realize that it's not one of those records where I went for two singles and then I put in a bunch of bad filler tracks. I worked my hardest on every song and picked the best twelve songs out of sixty-five songs that I wrote for this record over five years. So much blood, sweat, and tears have gone into it, and I'm definitely okay with people having their own opinion, whatever it is."

When Katy and Dr. Luke weren't working away in the studio, she and her team turned their attention to her image and style. Previous recording deals had failed with executives complaining about their inability to market the young singer. Her image was constantly coming into question. Just who was Katy Perry? She'd left Katy Hudson and her gospel roots behind when she moved to Los Angeles from Nashville. Now she was embracing the identity of a strong, feisty pop artist.

Luckily for Katy, her team at Capitol Records was supportive of her new image. As Bradford Cobb, her manager, said, "When Katy signed with Capitol, the direction they wanted to take was her direction."

Senior vice president Angelica Cob-Baehler remained one of Katy's biggest fans. Katy insisted on getting approval on how she was marketed, an attitude that Angelica supported. "I have people who are working with me who know exactly how I want to be portrayed, and my vision," said Katy in an interview. "You know . . . Me—Katy Perry—very sassy, cheeky, fun—cute, sexy, and smart."

Ur So Gay

Katy's first single was "Ur So Gay," an upbeat pop song that Katy wrote to mock the growing number of metrosexual men—guys who steal their girlfriends' eyeliner and are skinny enough to squeeze into their jeans.

Katy was writing from her life experience: "It's about those guys . . . [who] spend more time in the mirror than their girlfriends do. And I wrote it after bring dumped. It was one of the those relationships where the dumpage lasted longer than the actual relationship. . . ."

Rather than spend hours moping around after the breakup, Katy exacted revenge on her ex through music. She even told the guy—she played the song for him and announced that it was about him.

Her friends and boyfriends needed to watch out—it looked like anything they did could be inspiration behind a Katy Perry song. "I'm sure there is some fine print at the bottom of my life that says, 'Warning: if you date her, you might have your genitals cut off in a song,'" said Katy.

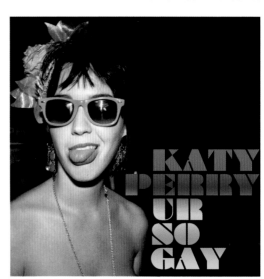

When asked in an interview about her debut single, Perry said the song was a "soft hello," which was why the plan was to release it online. The song "wasn't meant to be a big single or show what the album is going to be all about. That was for my Internet bloggers, so I'm not coming out of nowhere. 'UR So Gay' was meant to be an introduction and a background."

The song was produced and co-written by Greg Wells—a multiple Grammy-nominated musician, record producer, and songwriter—and was released on the Internet in November 2007. To accompany the song, Katy shot a video on a shoestring budget with her friend Walter May.

These were exciting times for Katy. She not only was about to release her first single with a major recording label, but she also had a new video to tell her friends about.

Katy blogged about it on MySpace, saying: "I think this video is very silly n' funny. My friend Walter and I were ichatting about wanting to do a little video for it a few weeks ago and I said let's use *Barbies*! (They're not official Barbies, thank the law!) Walter and team spray-painted, wall-papered and even *leathered* the miniature set . . . I hope you guys pick up on the funny little details . . . Like totally awesome rocker dude."

As the record company had no plans to release the song on the radio, it was never expected to be a commercial success. It did manage to pick up a few positive reviews, but, naturally, it failed to enter the *Billboard* Hot 100. However, it certainly launched Katy into the world—the media coverage was immense as people debated whether her song was offensive and homophobic.

"Every time I play that song, everybody has come back laughing," says Katy. "I'm not the type of person who walks around calling everything gay. That song is about a specific guy that I used to date and specific issues that he had. The song is about my ex wearing guyliner and taking emo pictures of himself in the bathroom mirror. The listeners have to read the context of the song and decide for themselves."

Katy spent weeks defending herself in the media, explaining: "It's not 'you're so gay,' like 'you're so lame'" said Katy, "I'm saying, 'You're so gay but I don't understand it because you don't like boys.'"

Katy became a worldwide phenomenon as her song was debated and discussed on news channels and in newspapers and magazines. Everyone knew who Katy Perry was, but, for the moment, she was just the girl with the "Gay" song. As it turned out, her next single would do little to dispel the media's curiosity about her and her sexuality. Just who was Katy Perry? Where had she come from, and who was she becoming? She was now a long way from her gospel roots and on the verge of the global stardom she had long dreamed of.

Opposite: Arriving in style at the 2008 MTV Video Music Awards in Los Angeles with celebrity blogger Perez Hilton.

Previous pages: Katy backstage during the 2008 Vans Warped Tour at the Pomona Fairgrounds.

MADONNA

By 2008, Katy was on the verge of erupting onto the music scene. Her first single for Columbia—"Ur So Gay"—was on the airwaves after her "soft launch." But the song's title and subject matter soon began to cause major controversy, leading to problems for both Katy and the record company.

As "Ur So Gay" received a large amount of airplay, it became a talking point around the globe, especially for gay rights activists. Katy was on the receiving end of a huge amount of criticism and accusations of homophobia, which rumbled on until a famous gay rights advocate declared her open support for the track and the tide turned—Katy was back on track and it was all down to Madonna.

In April 2008, Madonna was on the AZ KZZP–KRQQ radio show in Phoenix, Arizona, with JohnJay and Rich, and she was asked whether she had a song on her iPod that wasn't hers . . . Madonna's response? "Well, I have a favorite song right now," she said. "It's called 'Ur So Gay' and you don't even like boys." The hosts had never heard of Katy, so Madonna continued her tribute, saying: "Have you heard it? You have to hear it. It's by an artist Katy Perry. It's so good. Check it out on iTunes."

Katy couldn't believe it. Madonna had spoken. Furthermore, the global superstar and self-styled Queen of Pop didn't stop there. She continued her support for Katy, name-checking her again on one of America's most popular radio stations, KIIS-FM, when she was a guest on Ryan Seacrest's show. She insisting Seacrest "had to hear it," calling the song "hilarious."

Naturally, Katy was shocked. "It may have been a small comment on her behalf, but it was a large comment in my world," she said. "It was like a big boat leaving the dock and getting a champagne send-off."

Everyone was talking about Madonna's double shout-out for the previously unknown artist. With Madonna on Katy's side, people really started paying attention. Everywhere Katy went, she was asked about her latest fan.

In November 2008, Katy was interviewed by ITN news in the United Kingdom about her Madonna connections: "I was very nervous," said Katy. "Madonna, essentially every girl has her poster in their room . . . you go to bed, there's Madonna. You wake up looking at a poster of Madonna, and then all of a sudden, Madonna knows your first and last name and you're like 'Holy Crap,' I didn't expect it. She definitely gave me a nice compliment at the beginning of my career and maybe she doesn't remember who I am now. She's cool. I met her and she was very petite . . . I just thought of her as a giant my whole life." Naturally, at this stage of Katy's career, she had no idea how huge she herself was about to become as she continued to create hit after hit.

At one rock festival, cornered by an interviewer, Katy said: "I can't believe she knew my first and last name and she gave me such a great shout-out. It's one of those things . . . she really knew everything and I was so impressed that she knew me . . . I'm a new artist. I'm nobody. I'm just starting out and she has her finger on the pulse of what's going on and that's very cool."

At this early stage of her career, although she was known to a large number of music executives and producers, Katy was, to the general public anyway, as she said: "a nobody." So Madonna's knowledge of Katy's work was impressive and, by telling the world that this was her "favorite song," she opened a door that Katy was able to skip through.

By then, Katy was due to hit the road on the Vans Warped Tour, and declared to the world her long-term goal: "Ultimately," she said, "I want Katy Perry to be as much of a household name as Madonna." When she made this declaration she could have had little idea that she would actually achieve her goal—and all within eighteen months.

MADONNA IN A CORSET ON HER BLOND AMBITION TOUR, A LOOK THAT KATY HAS SINCE EMULATED.

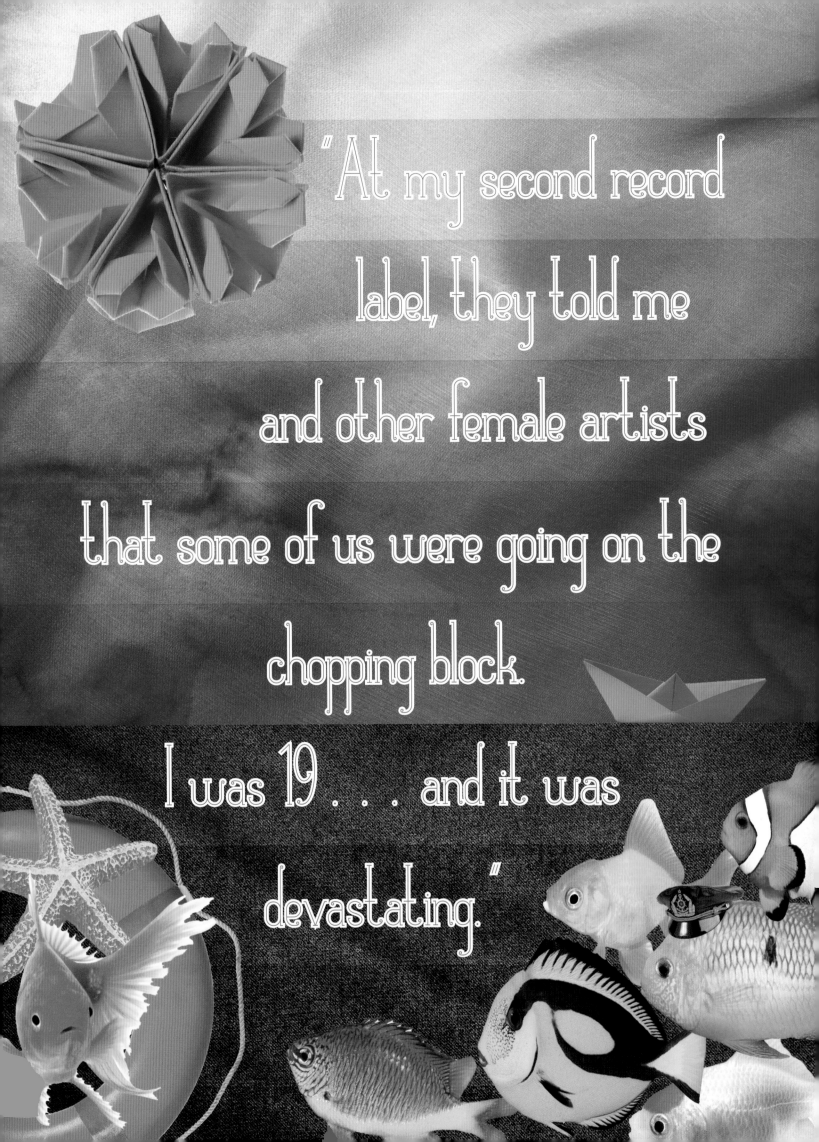

"At my second record label, they told me and other female artists that some of us were going on the chopping block. I was 19 . . . and it was devastating."

Breakthrough

Katy Perry will never forget 2008—it was the year that she truly exploded not only into the American charts but also across the world. Katy's big year kicked off in March with an appearance as herself on the ABC Family television series *Wildfire*. In an episode called "Life's Too Short," Katy sings "Thinking of You"—one of the upcoming songs on her soon-to-be-released album—in a nightclub. Because the show was mainly about the world of horse racing, it was a strange choice of ways to exhibit Katy's music, but she didn't really care—she was on television.

March also saw Katy perform at the prestigious SXSW (South by Southwest) Festival, one of the largest music festivals in the United States with around two thousand performers playing in more than ninety venues. On March 14 at 7:45 p.m., Katy got up on the stage, and sang as part of the ASCAP (American Society of Composers, Authors & Publishers) number. She was the first act and blew away the crowd as she played her own guitar and stood alone on the stage in a girly pink short dress.

"We were all blown away by her personality and talent when she played our showcase in SXSW in 2008," said Brendan Okrent, who signed Katy to ASCAP when she was nineteen. "Katy has continued to amaze us since with her incredible energy and innovation."

Everything was moving toward the release of Katy's single "I Kissed a Girl," the official lead single from her upcoming album *One of the Boys*. On May 6, 2008—two months after her SXSW performance—the single was released.

Katy had spent hours in a recording studio working on the track with Dr. Luke, Max Martin, and Cathy Dennis—all highly respected artists in the music industry. Max was a renowned Swedish music producer, who had worked with the Backstreet Boys, Britney Spears, and NSYNC. Cathy, a former pop icon herself, was the force behind many hits, including Kylie Minogue's "Can't Get You Out of My Head."

Katy was excited about "I Kissed a Girl." She had come up with the song after dreaming about it. She sat on the idea for eighteen months before deciding it was time. In an interview with the BBC, Katy said, "All of a sudden at the very, very end of making my album, I literally had two days left in the recording studio with my producer, Dr. Luke. We just said, 'We're gonna finish it—it's so catchy because it won't get out of our heads.'"

The first station to play the track was back in her former haunt of Nashville. The River, a popular station in Tennessee known for Top 40 music, played the song for a number of days, and, before long, the rest of the country had followed suit.

"I Kissed a Girl" debuted at number 76 on the *Billboard* Hot 100, but, soon afterward it was the number-one track in America. The song experienced commercial success domestically and internationally. It was number one at the top of the *Billboard* Hot 100 chart for seven consecutive weeks. It also made history by reaching the number one spot on *Billboard*'s Hot Dance Airplay chart by week three, a first for a solo act with a debut single. Katy made history in the United Kingdom where her song sold more than 635,000 copies—the first single for the label to do so since the Spice Girls' track "Goodbye" in 1998. When the song hit number one in the United States, it became the thousandth number-one song of the Rock Era (the 961st number one on the *Billboard* Hot 100).

Katy Perry had finally entered the ranks of pop stardom. Ultimately, "I Kissed a Girl" become a worldwide hit, topping the charts in more than twenty countries. Since its release, it has sold more than 4,155,000 digital copies in the United States alone. The song has since been recognized as the tenth best-selling single of the twenty-first century. Such was Katy's star status that, by September 2008, she was nominated in five categories at the MTV Video Music Awards, including Best New Artist. She might have lost out to Britney Spears that time, but everyone knew her name.

Opposite: Dressed to impress, Katy hosting the 2008 MTV Europe Music Awards ceremony in Liverpool.

"I want someone to tell the details to—that I had dinner with Paul McCartney or that I met Madonna, I'm on this extraordinary adventure, and if I have no one to talk to at the end of the night, I feel lonely."

Growing fame

On June 12, 2008, Katy appeared as herself on *The Young and the Restless*, one of America's most popular soap operas. In the episode, she is seen posing for the cover of the June 2008 issue of the fictional magazine *Restless Style*. From that point onward, the publicity juggernaut was in overdrive.

Katy also appeared on MTV's *Total Request Live*, *The Tonight Show with Jay Leno*, *Last Call with Carson Daly*, *The View*, *Howard Stern*, *So You Think You Can Dance*, and others. Thanks to the popularity of her latest single, Katy was getting a taste of the fame she'd always wanted.

Following the release of her album *One of the Boys*, Katy joined the Vans Warped Tour for its entire coast-to-coast run. From June 20 to August 17, Katy traveled cross-country alongside big-name punk rock acts such as Rise Against, The HorrorPops, The Vandals, and Pennywise. It was a great opportunity for her to get her music to a different crowd.

"Warped is going to be grueling and hot, but I'm ready to survive it—even without showers," Katy said. "Gwen Stefani did the tour back in 2000 with No Doubt and she looked fabulous hopping around on stage in her little polka-dotted dresses. I'm so channeling that."

"I'm excited and scared," Katy admitted. "The ratio of guys to girls is insane. I'm like trying to bring on as many girls as possible to the Warped Tour just so that I can have someone to lean on—and someone to crush on other guys with."

The tour started off in Katy's home state of California at the Fairplex Park in Pomona. "I'm eager to prove to people that even though I'm a pop artist on a major label, I'm legit," said Katy. "I play my guitar, and the band rocks, and I want to earn the respect of everybody out there."

Katy also had someone to share her journey with—Travie McCoy, lead singer of fellow Warped Tour act Gym Class Heroes. They had been casually dating for a while but would now be spending long hours together on the road.

"It's going to be a lot of self-control and keeping my eye on the prize," said Katy.

"But I have a boy that's going to be on the tour [and] I think we really like each other, so we'll see how that works."

Dating Travie certainly kept any unwelcome admirers at bay while she was on the Warped Tour. No one could get near her: "My boyfriend is 6'5" and covered in tattoos so I don't get a whole lot of attention from guys. They're pretty much scared shitless!"

Katy had met Travie a few years earlier in New York. "We were working with the same producer in New York City," said Katy, "At the end of my trip—it was just when I first started going to New York and not really knowing anybody—I was like, 'Please God, somebody take me out.' So I made him take me out. All of his friends were there, and we ended up dancing and making out on the dance floor." After hitting it off, they started tentatively dating long-distance—he stayed on the East Coast while she was back West. The Warped Tour was certainly going to be a test.

They spent ten weeks together during the festival, but, once it was over, they went back to their separate coasts. "It's definitely difficult," said Katy. "I was really lonely for a couple of weeks [after getting back to Los Angeles], but that's the name of the game. To me, iChat is the most beautiful technology invented, ever!"

As Katy's career soared, though, her relationship was proving harder to maintain due to the distance. Absence may make the heart grow fonder, but when your boyfriend is across the country, it's challenging to keep a relationship going, no matter how supportive and loving the intentions.

> My boyfriend is 6'5" and covered in *tattoos*, so I don't get a whole lot of *attention* from guys.

Katy backstage at the 2008 Vans Warped Tour at the Coors Amphitheater in San Diego.

Controversy strikes

Now that Katy was firmly in the public eye, she faced further scrutiny. Critics were investigating her past and discussing her evangelical parents as they tried to reconcile her Christian roots with her present-day pop temptress image. As Katy's profile grew, images from an old photo shoot became a transatlantic issue.

The publicity photo in question showed Katy posing with a switchblade and caused massive controversy in the United Kingdom. The picture was taken during a photo shoot with Terry Richardson in 2005, and featured Katy holding the knife close to her eye. It was done to give Katy a sexy, harder edge but was never used—and had supposedly disappeared. Until now.

As the criticism mounted, Katy was blamed for inciting violence and promoting weapons, which, of course, she wasn't. Friends who rallied to her side included musician Pete Wentz, from the band Fall Out Boy, who had been with her on the Warped tour. "It's absolutely ridiculous to compare that photo to somebody promoting violence," Wentz said.

Katy responded by releasing a picture of herself holding a spoon pressed to her cheek, with the following caption: "I don't condone knife use, but I do condone eating ice-cream with a very large spoon."

"It wasn't something I was trying to hide," said Katy at the time. "I'm a pop girl and I wanna make people happy so it hurt me to be connected to something that really is a big deal." The controversy was huge and there was even talk of Katy being dropped as a cohost for the MTV Europe Music Awards that year. In the event, that didn't happen and she was a shining light at the ceremony. She even picked up the prize for Best New Act.

As Christian pastors, Katy's parents were now also in the spotlight, with people wanting to know how they felt about their daughter strutting on stages all across the world singing "I Kissed a Girl."

"My parents are definitely supportive and happy for my success," said Katy. "I think if they did it their way, then maybe I wouldn't be singing a song with this subject matter, but I'm an adult, I make my own decisions now." But, were her parents really that surprised by Katy? She had always gone her own way, after all. "It was more like, Katy's always had something to say, now she's saying . . . this."

It looked like there were plenty of people waiting to cash in on the Katy Perry phenomenon. In August of 2008, Katy's former collaborators the Matrix released the album that they'd worked with Katy on in 2004. "To be honest, we had a much earlier release date planned," said Matrix member Lauren Christy. "We had the dates set up with iTunes . . . and then 'I Kissed a Girl' exploded," Christy said. "I spoke to Katy about it, and she wanted to wait until the fourth single off her album was released. . . . We don't want to be pop stars, and we're not releasing it on a major label. And it's not called 'Katy Perry and the Matrix.' These are just great songs, and I'm very proud of it." The album was released under their own record label, Let's Hear It Records.

Everyone wanted Katy. In September, she sang "I Kissed a Girl" and Madonna's "Like a Virgin" at the MTV Video Music Awards. In October, she performed at the Premios MTV Latinoamérica. She was on the cover of *Blender*'s November 2008 issue.

In the same month she dressed up as a flamenco dancer to strut her stuff at the Ondas Awards in Barcelona, Spain, before taking part in a new Adidas advertisement alongside David Beckham, Missy Elliot, and other celebrities to mark the company's "60 Years of Soles and Stripes."

Katy was certainly on a roll professionally, but by December her personal life was falling apart. After three years of dating, she and Travie broke up—the distance between them had proved too much to overcome.

As fate would have it, Katy spent New Year's Eve in Travie's home city of New York, but he was the last thought on her mind. She was one of the acts—alongside Ludacris and 50 Cent—seeing out the year by performing songs from her now-gold album *One of the Boys* on NBC's *New Year's Eve with Carson Daly*. It had been a year that gave Katy everything she could have wished for, but there was still more to come.

On September 9, 2008, Katy's second official single "Hot N Cold" was released in the United States. Its success followed in the wake of "I Kissed a Girl" and would go on to seal her status as a worldwide pop star.

Katy's second hit single was a truly bicoastal effort as Katy had worked on it with Dr. Luke & Max Martin in both Dr. Luke's Legacy Recording Studio in New York City and the Conway Recording Studio in Hollywood. Although the single didn't have the phenomenal success of "I Kissed a Girl," it was still a worldwide hit, reaching number three on the *Billboard* Hot 100.

"Hot N Cold" was one of the most promoted songs on the U.S. airwaves for weeks as it blasted out of radios up and down the country. As one reviewer wrote: "With a disco feel to it, "Hot N Cold" is certainly one of the most ear- catching songs on [Katy's album] *One of the Boys*. Katy Perry has a reputation for wacky dressing and lavish videos, and "Hot N Cold" finds her jilted at the altar, only to track down the offender with a hoard of bridal dress wearing, baseball bat wielding maniacs." It had a dramatic theme, which allegedly was a nod to Katy's now ex-boyfriend Travis McCoy.

The song peaked at number three on the Hot 100 on November 22, making it her second top-three hit. It stayed in the top ten for eighteen weeks and went on to be a certified four-times-platinum by the RIAA. With digital sales now in excess of five million copies, "Hot N Cold" turned out to be the best-selling single of her career in the U.S., despite never reaching number one. In Canada, the song reached number one on the charts in November 2008. Ultimately it was an even bigger radio hit than "I Kissed a Girl" as it was Katy's first number one on both U.S. Mainstream Top 40 and Adult Top

40 radio charts. As of September 2011, the song had sold more than 5,011,000 digital downloads in the United States.

Along with Katy's success, her music was infiltrating popular culture across the globe. The song was used in a commercial promoting an Australian soap opera, *Out of the Blue* and became the theme music for *MasterChef Australia* and the associated TV ads. "Hot N Cold" was also featured in the opening sequence for the 2009 film *The Ugly Truth* starring Katherine Heigl and Gerard Butler and in the trailer for the 2009 film *The Proposal* starring Sandra Bullock and Ryan Reynolds.

It also received airplay on the TV shows *Ghost Whisperer* and *90210*, and the list goes on. It was played in the seventh instalment of the *American Pie* franchise film *American Pie Presents: The Book of Love* and was sung by a group of high school boys at the beginning of *This American Life* episode 395, "Middle of the Night." A cover version in the fictional language of "Simlish" was used in the video game *The Sims 2* on the radio station Pop and the song featured in the 2011 film *Mean Girls 2*, a sequel to the 2004 film *Mean Girls*.

Finally, the single was nominated for the 52nd Grammy Awards in the category of Best Female Pop Vocal Performance. Katy Perry was firmly on the map.

Katy and friends at the release party for her *One of the Boys* album in 2008.

Pop star feud

No fully-fledged pop star these days can be complete without a media-fueled feud and, by December 2008, Katy had her very own public spat with British pop artist Lily Allen. It started with one casual comment from Katy, which brought on months of traded insults that, needlesss to say, appeared in publications across the globe.

The "feud" started in June 2008, thanks to a blog by Katy's supporter and friend Perez Hilton, a well-known American television personality and blogger who covers gossip items on celebrities. Hilton blogged: "And the battle is on! It's hard to stay on top in the music industry. Just ask Lily Allen! Lily used to be Capitol Records' 'golden girl,' but lately she's been slipping. She's known these days more for being a tragic train wreck than a musician. She knows it, too. That must hurt! And now it seems she's been replaced. Replaced by none other than a Perez fav, Katy Perry, which we first introduced you to last year."

His blog continued, asserting that Katy had replaced Lily as their main star, and that Lily's photo, which had allegedly hung in the lobby of the Capitol Records office, had been replaced by Katy's image. Perez didn't stop sticking the knife in, as he then went on to insult Lily's music-writing: "But, from what we're hearing, Lily's new material s-u-c-k-s."

At this stage, of course, Katy had nothing to do with the drama, it was between Perez and Lily, who decided to respond via her MySpace page, saying: "I don't know why this has annoyed me so much. If I'm honest, it's probably because part of it is true, these days I am more known for being a train wreck than a musician, and it does hurt. I've been working really hard on my new record; I don't think it sucks by the way." She pointed out that she was signed to Regal Records in the United Kingdom while Capitol distributed her records in America. Furthermore, she explained she had only been to Capitol's New York office once, and that it would be unlikely they would have a photo of her.

The blogging and posting between the pair continued for a while, all played out in the public arena. Katy must have been aware of it, but she was, at the time, more concerned with the release of her second single "Hot N Cold."

Six months later, just when it looked like the feud was over, a casual comment by Katy stirred up the old rivalry between the pair. Katy, foolishly, described herself on MySpace in the "sounds like" section as a "fatter version of Amy Winehouse and a skinnier version of Lily Allen."

Lily, naturally, was furious. On December 8, the war between the two was reignited when Lily said, live on the UK radio station Capital FM, "I happen to know for a fact that she was an American version of me. She was signed by my label in America as, 'We need to find something controversial and kooky like Lily Allen.' And then they found her. I think the lyrics and stuff are a bit crass."

A day later, while filming a Fuse TV show, Katy was asked to respond to Lily's comments, and stated that her remarks were only meant to be a joke.

"Yeah, I made a joke about [that] earlier this year," Katy said. "I was just kind of joking and trying to be funny. I didn't mean anything by it. Comedians are not necessarily to be taken super seriously."

Despite Katy's explanation that her comments were just a joke, the feud continued into the New Year. In January 2009, it was reported that Lily threatened she would post Katy's phone number on Facebook.

Katy, on the whole, rarely discussed the childish "feud," but she did make one comment to the *Herald Sun* newspaper in Australia, saying: "We are both quite different. She's got the cool, reggae, laid-back sensibility with kooky lyrics and a great sense of humor. My stuff is a little more rock and pop and somewhat more mainstream. I think we both have different things to offer. Is there bad blood? Not from me. I will continue to buy her records. She's actually looking great these days, pretty fit." With that interview, it seemed like the feud was finally put to rest. For now.

"I don't take anything for granted. There are 5 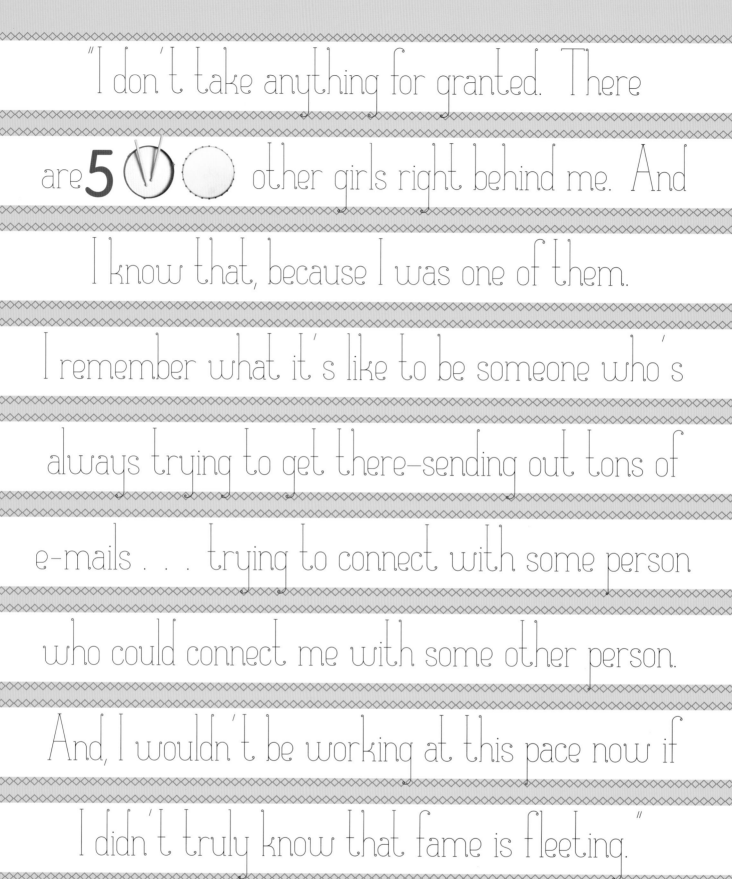 other girls right behind me. And I know that, because I was one of them. I remember what it's like to be someone who's always trying to get there—sending out tons of e-mails . . . trying to connect with some person who could connect me with some other person. And, I wouldn't be working at this pace now if I didn't truly know that fame is fleeting."

Surviving awards season

After the successes of 2008 with her two singles "I Kissed a Girl" and "Hot N Cold," now came the awards and the accolades. Katy couldn't be more excited—her dreams were coming true.

As Katy said: "A lot of people are like "Ugh, pop music." Or major record labels think it's cool to be Indie but my dream as a little girl was to be on the Grammys and to have my record be available to everyone in the whole world. That's why I need that big record label."

Katy was traveling the world, attending award show after award show and performing. Naturally, wherever she went, there was usually some drama behind her. In fact, in October 2008, at MTV's Latin America Awards in Guadalajara, Mexico, Katy was meant to merely dive into a giant cake at an awards party, but instead she slipped on the icing, fell, and hit the ground covered in cream. It made for some great candid photo opportunities and, of course, free publicity.

In February 2009, both "I Kissed a Girl" and "Hot N Cold" were certified three-time platinum by the Recording Industry Association of America for individual digital sales of over three million. In fact, February proved to be one of Katy's busiest months.

On February 8, 2009, Katy was nominated for the Grammy Awards, fulfilling the dreams of her childhood. She was up for Best Female Pop Vocal Performance. At the time she said: "If I was a twelve-year-old kid and pushed 'record' and had my video appear on the Grammys as I'm sitting there eating popcorn, I would have fainted. [I would have been] blown away!"

Katy was also due to perform at the event and, of course, she was preparing quite a spectacle, fueling speculation before the event about the staging of the show.

"I'm going to be ascending from the ceiling," she told MTV News at the Clive Davis Pre-Grammy Gala. "By banana!" She was also planning to include some retro choreography in her routine. "It's a little 1940s Folies Bergère/Rockette [style]," she explained. "It's definitely not [like Britney Spears' 2001 VMA performance of] "I'm a Slave 4 U" or something like that. No anacondas on my neck. It's definitely hopefully going to be one of those moments."

She spent weeks preparing for the show, saying, "I've been getting my rest and doing rehearsal," she said. "I'm nervous! I have this little sick-to-my-stomach feeling. I think it's a healthy feeling." It seems the neves paid off as everything went well on the night and the show was a huge success."

Just ten days later, the singer was in London for the Brit Awards. The ceremony is the British version of the Grammy Awards and one of the highest accolades in the music industry. The show that year was watched by 5.49 million people and Katy was up for International Female Solo Artist.

Lionel Richie was presenting the award and when he called out the name "Katy Perry," her table immediately started celebrating as she made her way to the stage. Looking flustered, Katy held up the award and said: "Holy Shit!" She held up the award. "I just want to thank everyone here in London and everyone in the UK. I'm so sick right now. But they said I should show up to the Brits because something special might happen. Thank you so much. Thank all of you. Thank you everyone at my record label who have worked so hard and obviously I've worked pretty hard too because I want to die right now."

Katy didn't die, but when she left the stage, she was horribly and physically sick.

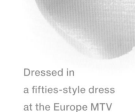

Dressed in a fifties-style dress at the Europe MTV music awards 2009.

Hello Katy

Never one to be scared of hard work, Katy had been practicing her craft since her first singing lesson at nine years of age back in her hometown of Santa Barbara. The success she was now enjoying was the result of all the hard graft over the years.

Even though her Hello Katy Tour meant a grueling ten months of traveling, it was everything Katy had been working toward since starting out. The tour was set up to promote her debut album, *One of the Boys*, with the first show scheduled for January 23, 2009, in Seattle, Washington.

When asked what to expect on her first solo tour, Perry stated: "We're preparing for a fun, eye-candy-filled show, with great musicianship and basically, leaving people with a 'what the [expletive] was that?' feeling."

Touring North America, Asia, Europe, and Australia gave Katy the chance to indulge her dream of putting on a huge show and getting her music out to the entire world. She packed professionals on to her tour and set off on the road: "I have the guy who creates stages for Madonna working on this tour," said Katy. "I'm indulging my obsession with fruit and cats and designing all different outfits."

Just before she went on tour, Katy gave an interview to the *Seattle Times*—the first stop on the tour—in which she talked about her need to ensure that she could give her fans what they wanted, "I'm a goofball, but I'm a professional goofball. . . . I understand the responsibility I have and the opportunity I have, that so many people want these days and it's really hard to come by. I think people, or at least the hard-core fans, are expecting me to continually impress them and I will. I will try to because I'm in a constant competition with myself."

Just before her opening show in Seattle, Katy got the flu, and many worried that she wouldn't be able to go on with the show. Yet, as everyone would discover, Katy is a fighter, and there was no way she was going to miss out on the opportunity to perform. "I knew I had the responsibility to get healthy really fast, so I could rehearse and put on a great show and have a fantastic tour."

The show opened with the song "California Girls" by the Beach Boys playing as Katy hit the stage to belt out songs such as "Fingerprints," "One of the Boys," "Self Inflicted" and "Mannequin." During her performances, Katy spent time "talking" to the audience—at one stage she did the "Hokey Pokey," telling the fans that the dance is like having a relationship, having "one foot in, and one foot out." Considering that Katy had just broken up with her boyfriend of three years, Travie McCoy, it seemed like she was making a comment on their relationship.

> We're preparing for a fun, *eye-candy-filled* show with great musicianship. . . .

As the year went on, Katy was becoming more popular, and the crowds were getting bigger as her reputation increased. "I feel like I've been on tour since it's been happening, which is awesome," said Katy.

While performing, Katy would look out at the audiences and see her fans—at times it was overwhelming. "I get to see the crowds grow and people get more excited. One girl fainted. It was crazy. I was like, 'Chill out! It's just me!' This morning I was in Milan and a couple of mornings before that I was in Germany and London and Paris. I'm zigzagging all over Europe. Then, for like seventeen days, I'm in Australia, New Mexico, and Japan. It's incredibly hectic but there are no complaints."

The tour proved to be highly successful and put Katy on the map. When asked about it, Katy responded with laughter: "Oh yeah, I sold out my whole tour! I'm a sell-out in the most positive way! But no, I don't think I'm a sell-out at all. I like to go big! I love pop music. I'm not ashamed, you know?"

A sold-out tour and hits galore—and it all took place over the course of one year.

In 2009 Katy traveled the world, appearing onstage wherever she went.

LOLITA

n 1997, when Katy was thirteen, a new film version of *Lolita* was released. Directed by Adrian Lyne, the film stars Dominique Swain as a young girl called Lolita and Jeremy Irons as Humbert Humbert, an older man with whom she becomes sexually involved. Based on the controversial but popular Vladimir Nabokov novel, first published in 1955, the story explores themes of a young girl's burgeoning sexuality. Katy later also saw the earlier film version, directed by Stanley Kubrick in 1962. However, it was Dominique Swain's style in the 1997 film that really caught Katy's eye and has remained an influence ever since.

It's highly unlikely that either the book or the two films would have been popular choices at home growing up—given how discriminating Katy's parents were of all reading and viewing material in their religious household. If channels such as VH1 and MTV were banned, the book *Lolita* certainly wouldn't have crossed the threshold as acceptable reading material.

Despite her parents' strict rules, however, Katy came across both the book and the films. Many years later, when releasing the title song of her album *One of the Boys*, she said she had "studied Lolita religiously," that it was one of her favorite books. Such was her appreciation of the story that the cover shot of the album referenced Lolita's appearance in the earlier Kubrick film.

"When we shot the record cover," said Katy, "I took a picture of Lolita, y'know, her sprawled out on the front porch with her kind-of-like American-hot-summer-sex-kitten-still-innocent-and-naïve-but-knows-exactly-what-she's-doing picture. Lolita is kind of f**ked up. [But] off the bat, I never said, 'Hey, check me out, this is the way you should live your

> "I have this weird obsession with her. . . . I am obsessed with how she can straddle the line of being innocent and sexy all in one"

life.' I never said, 'You should have sex at the same age I had sex.' Whether you like it or not, girls of that age [14] are thinking about boys. We're getting our hearts crushed and having our first relationships. Hopefully some of my songs can help them get over or deal with it."

Katy was a fan of both versions of *Lolita* and, when asked about it, said: "It's my favorite movie in the world. I have this weird obsession with her. I love the Kubrick movie, but I also love the other movie with Jeremy Irons and Dominique Swain. I've been obsessed with that movie for years now. I just got a soft pink Gibson Les Paul and I named it Lolita."

It's not just her guitar that gets the "Lolita" treatment. Her love of *Lolita* was also apparent at the 2009 Annual Grammy Awards. Katy chose to channel her inner *Lolita* and admitted that some of her onstage costumes were inspired by Dominique Swain.

Katy describes her unconventional fashion style as "a bit of a concoction of different things." She has also said: "I have my own look, which I call 'Lolita meets old Hollywood Glam.'" But she struggles to explain why she's so obsessed. "Well, it's just weird," said Katy about her love of *Lolita*. "I mean, I'm obsessed. I'm obsessed with how she can straddle the line of being innocent and sexy all in one. She's a beautiful creature, very girlie, sweet, and innocent, but she knows exactly what she's doing, you know?"

Katy finds these themes fascinating because she identifies with the mixture of innocence and sexiness: "To me, I see a lot of myself like that. I am still sweet and a girl-next-door, and I'm a good girlfriend. I think that I straddle the line a little bit because I know that I also am a bit of a tiger."

ONE OF KATY'S STYLE ICONS IS LOLITA, SEEN HERE IN THE 1997 FILM VERSION. ☞

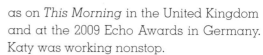

Chart dipper

When Katy wasn't on tour, appearing on the festival circuit, or hosting award ceremonies, she was promoting her latest releases from *One of the Boys*. In early 2009, Katy had two singles released in quick succession. The first was "Thinking of You," released in the United States in January 2009, while the next was "Waking Up in Vegas," which came out in April.

"Thinking of You," which was written solely by Katy herself, became her lowest charting single worldwide. It was her only song to not break the Top 10, peaking at number 29 on the *Billboard* Hot 100 chart, number 27 in the United Kingdom, and number 34 on the Canadian Singles Chart—though it still managed to be certified platinum by the Canadian Recording Industry Association. For an artist as successful as Katy had become, her team was hoping this was merely a blip.

In Europe, Katy Perry fans remained loyal, and the song received moderate success. It debuted at number 63 on the UK Singles Chart, peaking at number 27 after seven weeks. The song reached number 38 on the Irish Singles Chart, and in France, it debuted at number 11 on the singles chart and stayed on the chart for 32 weeks, becoming Katy's longest-charting single there. As of September 2011, the song has sold 953,000 downloads in the United States which, considering its slow start, is incredibly impressive.

The song was promoted worldwide. It was featured on the soundtrack to *India: A Love Story*, a Brazilian telenova. Katy performed the song on *The Ellen DeGeneres Show*, *The Early Show*, and *Last Call with Carson Daly*, as well

as on *This Morning* in the United Kingdom and at the 2009 Echo Awards in Germany. Katy was working nonstop.

Despite the song's low positioning on the charts, the BBC gave it a positive review: "'Thinking of You' is a four-minute plus ballad which laments the end of a relationship, and it seems that Katy's true voice shines through here. On some tracks, it feels like she's doing songs 'in the style of,' but on this song you can hear an edge and a rawness that makes you feel like you're finally listening to the real Katy."

On April 21, 2009, "Waking Up in Vegas"—Katy's fourth and final single from *One of the Boys*—was officially released to U.S. radio stations.

In the main, the song was well received by music critics and did better than her previous single, peaking at number nine on the *Billboard* Hot 100. It was Katy's third Top 10 single on the charts. The song also reached number one in Australia and The Netherlands, while making it to the Top 10 in Canada, New Zealand, and Italy.

According to sources in the Perry camp, "Waking Up in Vegas" was a key track in her career. It was one of the songs she had recorded while still under contract with Columbia Records, and apparently, it was one of three songs circulating around Capitol Records as an example of Katy's capabilities. It worked—years after having been recorded, the song soared up the charts when it was released.

Before "Waking Up in Vegas" was released, "If You Can Afford Me" and "Fingerprints" had been considered for release, but Katy chose Vegas instead. "Vegas gives me that 'what the f***' feeling," said Katy. "It's really close to L.A. so one night you could be having a beer with your friends and, when you wake up, you're in Vegas."

Katy added that the song is not about apologizing: "[It's] basically a song about getting into trouble with your best friend or your boyfriend or your girlfriend—or whoever you're with—and not having any 'I'm sorry for what I did.'" It certainly proved to be a winner—selling more than 2,053,000 copies in the U.S.

When Katy met Katie

Previous pages:
Getting slimed at
the Nickelodeon
Kids' Choice
Awards.

Opposite: A
bemused-looking
Katy at the Grammy
Nominations
Concert Live!
in 2009.

In June 2009, Katy had a new drama to deal with—another Katie Perry was causing headaches for her legal team. Katie Perry, a luxury loungewear designer in Australia, had the misfortune of having a name similar to Katy's. In a bid to protect Katy's growing popularity and public image, Katy's lawyers served Katie a cease-and-desist order as they aimed to stop her from trademarking her birth name for her clothing label.

Katie Perry, a native of Australia, had set up a fashion label under her own name. In 2007, she had plans to open her first retail outlet store in a suburb of Sydney and filed

> She wasn't just an American pop star, Katy Perry was a *worldwide phenomenon.... contantly under scrutiny*

paperwork to trademark her name for both the store and her line. It was this act that drew attention from Katy's lawyers. The fashion designer was shocked to receive a letter from a legal firm acting on behalf of Katy—asking her to stop selling her line.

The story broke in the Antipodean newspaper *The Australian* and featured several quotes from Katie Perry about her distress regarding the legal document. Katie said: "I got such a huge shock. It really felt like I was being intimidated and bullied into signing

everything away. It asked me to give up the trademark, withdraw sales of my clothes, withdraw any advertising and any websites and sign that I will not, in the future, use a similar trademark to Katy Perry. I pretty much burst into tears. I love my business. I'm not going to give it away without a fight, either. I'm not trying to become a singer. I'm not pretending to be her. This is my income. And it's the livelihood of my contractors as well."

The Australian also quoted trademark lawyer Trevor Choy, who commented that it was no surprise that Katy had opposed the trademark application, as singers (such as J-Lo and Gwen Stefani) frequently launch their own fashion labels. "A lot of U.S. pop stars are moving into all sorts of merchandising," Mr Choy said. "Clothing is an obvious one for pop stars. The fact that it's [Australian Katie Perry's] birth name doesn't necessarily change things dramatically. It means they can't stop her from using it but she can't necessarily get protection over it."

Katie blogged furiously about her frustrations on her website and thanked fashion fans for their support: "The moment the article in *The Australian* came out I have been inundated form [sic] support from across the world. . . . Having always studied and worked in the fashion industry this label is my dream and to have [it] threatened to be taken away from me has been devastating. A lot of people have been asking how they can support me."

Katy, in return, blogged that there was no lawsuit between the two, merely that her lawyers sent a notice letter to Katie Perry. Back in Australia, on July 18, 2009, Katie Perry posted a picture of herself on her personal blog, stating, "Its [sic] all over!!!" She went on to say: "The battle against my trademark has finished with the withdrawal of opposition from the singer, Katy Perry's lawyers. It is amazing to think that it is all over. There have been MANY learnings [sic] from this experience, all of which I wish I could have learnt in another way!!!"

Ultimately, the case died away, becoming a mere footnote in Katy Perry's story, but it was a clear indication of how her team was already fiercely protecting her global assets. She wasn't just an American pop star, Katy Perry was a worldwide phenomenon, whose reputation and commercial viability was now constantly under scrutiny.

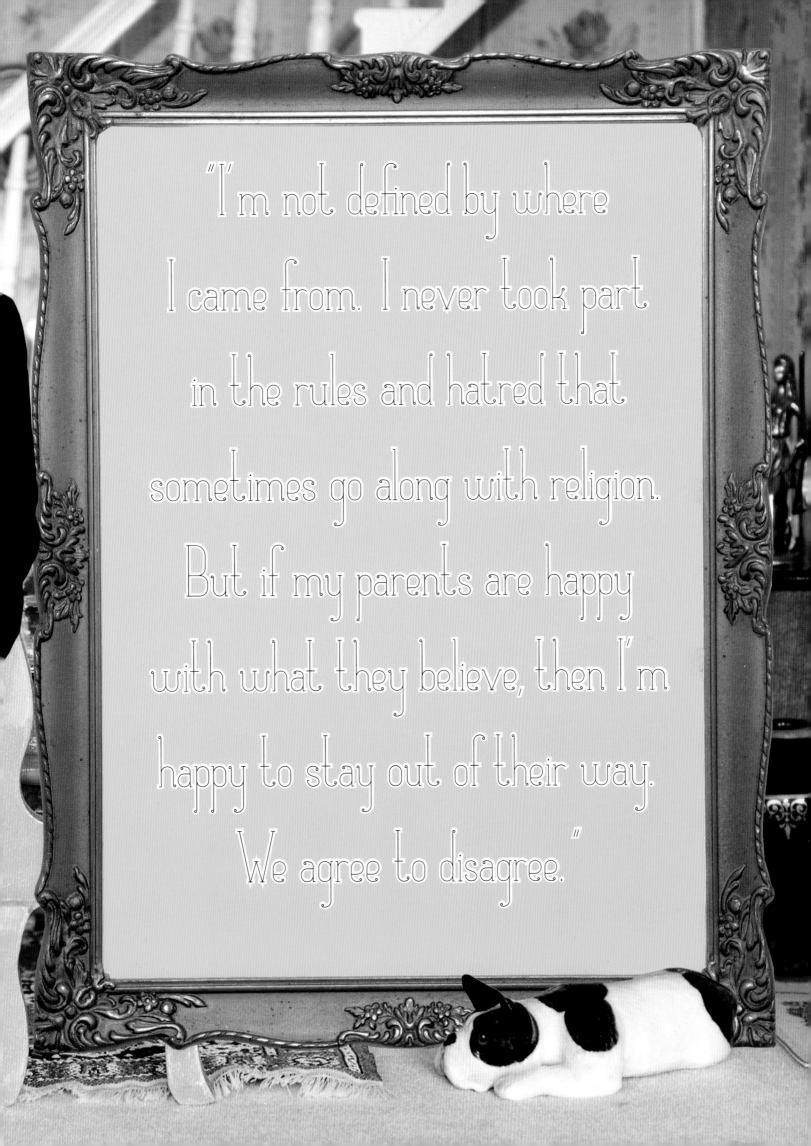

"I'm not defined by where I came from. I never took part in the rules and hatred that sometimes go along with religion. But if my parents are happy with what they believe, then I'm happy to stay out of their way. We agree to disagree."

I'm *nervous!* I have this little *sick-to-my-stomach* feeling. I think it's a healthy feeling.

Branded woman

During 2008 and 2009, Katy Perry and Russell Brand were dancing around each other. There was an obvious attraction between them, but neither of them followed through. When the pair first met, Katy was dating Travie McCoy, but that hadn't stopped the sparks from flying.

Katy and Russell first met in September 2008 at the MTV Video Music Awards. After her phenomenal success with "I Kissed a Girl," Katy was nominated for several awards, and the man who was going to be her future husband, Russell, was hosting the event. Comedian Russell was a relative newcomer to the celebrity scene in the United States where he was in the process of launching his American career. Katy, on the other hand, was the star. Although virtually unknown just a year before, that night she was nominated for five awards.

All eyes were on the pop star as she took to the stage to sing her number-one hit, after which Russell joked: "I was so inspired by Katy Perry's song's message that I'm currently going through nine ChapSticks a day and my penis has never felt more moisturized."

Also at the VMAs, director Nicholas Stoller was setting up a shoot to capture celebrity cameos for Russell's upcoming film *Get Him to the Greek*. Stars such as Christina Aguilera, Pink, and Katy were due to be in the film. As it turned out, Katy's kiss with Russell was cut from the final version of the film, but Katy was able to joke about it.

Never one to hold back, Katy discussed the cheeky Brit, declaring in a radio interview shortly after the VMAs: "I met Russell Brand, who I'm in love with. I love him, he's so great. He's got the worst sense of humor in the best sense of the way."

In a 2010 interview, Katy discussed their immediate attraction: "When [Russell] was filming *Get Him to the Greek*, I did a cameo with him. My scene called for me to make out with him. And on the way down the stairs after the scene, I was hopping like a bunny. I hop like a bunny when I'm happy—I get a bit childlike."

There was one major problem standing in their way—she was still dating Gym Class Heroes frontman Travie McCoy, and Katy wasn't going to cheat on her man. By December 2008, however, Travie and Katy ended their relationship, but Katy and Russell didn't reconnect immediately. Having spent three years with Travie, it was going to take a while for Katy to get back into a new relationship, and she was working like crazy. So, it wasn't a surprise to her friends when, six months later, Travie and Katy briefly reunited.

At the time, Travie said: "The break-up sucked. . . . I keep thinking about if I had to go through it again and how terrible it would be. We were moving way too fast. I was being juvenile about the entire thing. Now it's easy breezy. I'm happy and really in love." Sadly, it didn't last and, by September of 2009, Katy Perry was single and ready to meet up with Russell Brand again.

For a second time, MTV played Cupid for the duo. On September 13, 2009, it was time for the VMAs, and Russell was hosting the show again. The

pair flirted throughout rehearsals and even during the show, which Katy opened with a rousing rendition of one of her favorite Queen songs, "We Will Rock You," before Russell took to the stage.

After the show, both Russell and Katy were all hyped up, and, according to witnesses, the two were passionately kissing in a corner at the after-party. By all accounts, the relationship heated up fairly quickly. By October, the pair was spotted together at a Fendi party during Paris Fashion Week— they were officially a couple. Despite Katy's grueling schedule, the duo did their best to keep their relationship alive. Unlike in her previous long-distance relationship with Travie, both Russell and Katy were making every effort to make this one work.

Always on the move

After Katy and Russell started dating, the pair struggled to make time together as Katy was constantly on the move. She was traveling all over the world, playing at nearly every prominent music festival as the Perry bandwagon maintained momentum.

In June 2009, Katy was in London for a concert at Shepherd's Bush Empire, receiving rave reviews for her performance. *The Observer* wrote: "Perry shines when she performs live and the goofy, rude persona that has come through in the press, lyrics, and videos is incredibly likable on stage. . . . Perry's real magic comes from what so many singers lack: her personality. Perry, at 24, is still teenager-rude—laconic, with a biting wit and level of cheek usually only heard from the back row of a classroom."

From July onward, Katy racked up the air miles. After London, she crossed the Atlantic again for an August 2 show at the Verizon Wireless Theater in downtown Houston, Texas. It was a gig she couldn't miss—she had stood them up twice before and couldn't let her fans down again.

"Oh, goodness gracious, the first time I was so sick," said Katy. "I couldn't even move. The second time, I had *American Idol*, and I had all this pressure from everybody. I couldn't make the flight or something. I had to move Houston or drop *American Idol* and, like, lose my career. People freak out for these opportunities."

By August, Katy was off to Australia and, over the course of six days, she performed in Brisbane, Melbourne, and Sydney to even more positive reviews. One wrote: "Katy Perry rocked Melbourne . . . and we liked it!" Another raved about her Sydney show: "The Enmore Theatre stage was decorated with flamingos and giant strawberries and a small white picket fence. When the band arrived they were in pink suits and Katy Perry bounced out in a glittery high-waisted shorts and cropped-top ensemble that resembled a 1950s bikini. In fact, with her black wavy locks atop this combination, Perry had a touch of Jane Russell poolside from *Gentlemen Prefer Blondes*."

From here, Katy faced a three-flight, 26-hour journey from Australia to Scotland, where she was due to perform another rescheduled gig at Barrowland in Glasgow. So, when security at the airport insisted on checking her five cases, Katy was so rundown and frustrated that she ended up having a public meltdown.

She was exhausted, and the press had a field day commenting on her outburst. In an interview after the incident Katy said: "I swear, I never feel more like cattle than when I have to go through airport security. They hate their lives and they hate us for sure. By the last flight, the third time going through security, I lost it on a security person."

When Katy arrived at her hotel in Glasgow, she told an interviewer, "I am so tired. I'm not even sure if I'll be venturing out today. All I want right now is a shower and then my bed."

She didn't have long to relax, and after the show, she headed for England and the V Festival at Chelmsford.

A hugely popular music festival, the V is held on the second-to-last weekend in August. In 2009, there were around 20,000 fans listening to Katy as she strapped on a white guitar to play "One of the Boys" and jokingly sniffed her armpit after singing the line "I want to smell like roses, not a baseball team."

Katy announced to the crowd that her V Festival shows were going to be among her last before heading back into the studio to record a follow-up to *One of the Boys*.

"I feel like I'm in the eye of the hurricane. There is so much going on around me," she said. "But I have learned the art of self control and really have had to grow up a ton this year and figure out what the word 'priority' means—getting to bed and not drinking and remembering that the party will always be there."

By September, Katy was back in New York City, at Radio City Hall for the Video Music Awards. There, she found herself back in Russell Brand's arms as their relationship really began in earnest.

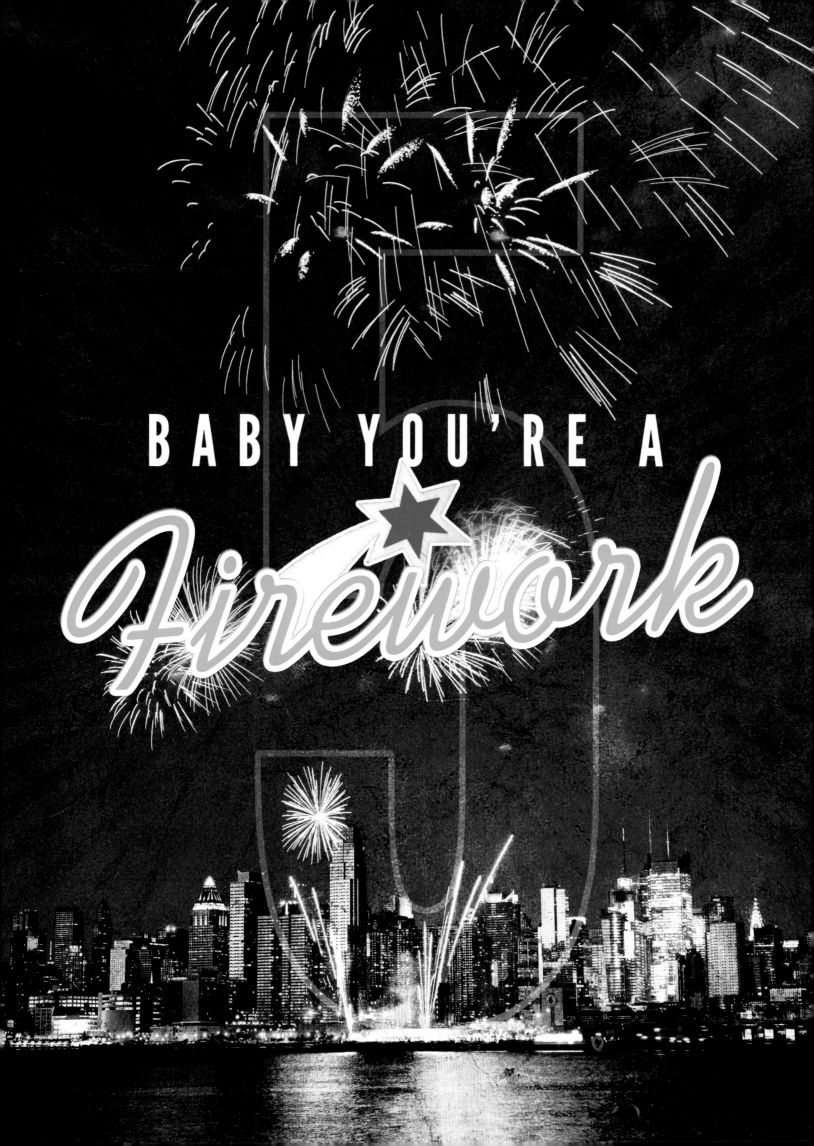

Following the VMAs in September 2009, Katy and Russell were rarely apart, and with daily contact by text or Twitter, it seemed their romance was being played out in the public arena.

"Everything clicked really fast," Katy said. "We kind of instantly got past all the surfacey stuff." In fact, on their first date, Russell gave her a necklace with black diamond beads—extraordinarily extravagant, but it showed the Englishman was serious about wooing the California girl.

In October, Russell and Katy disappeared to Thailand together. Katy tweeted about the getaway: "After a week in magical Thailand I'm ready to face the real world again. Been schooled on Morrissey, Oscar Wilde & Peter Sellers . . . inspired."

Katy claimed that she was unaware of Russell's past as a rapacious womanizer and former heroin addict. "I guess I had heard faintly of his reputation, and his hairdo, but there's a lot of stuff that goes on in the English press and entertainment world that never makes it to the States," she said. "We both needed balance, and we give that to each other. It wasn't about me taming him, which is what everyone always says—it was about timing."

To celebrate her twenty-fifth birthday (on October 25), Katy turned The Beach restaurant in Los Angeles into Willy Wonka's famous sweet factory, filled with giant lollipops and candy. Her family and friends—such as Taylor Swift and P. Diddy—were there to help her celebrate. Katy's relationship with Russell was blossoming. They arrived at her birthday celebration holding hands as a couple.

A month later, in November, Katy had the honor of hosting the MTV Europe Music Awards in Berlin. It was a huge deal for the singer. "I'm just going to be myself," Katy said at the press conference the day before the show. "MTV asked me back because I have this no fear attitude. I don't care if I do fall over or if a boob does fall out! I'm

highlighting what God gave me. Using what your mama made! Last year I was all bright and fruity, but now we're in Berlin it's going to be all sexy, dark and romantic with a cabaret undertone."

Always one to put on a show for her audience, this time Katy also put on a show for Russell. She performed a number wearing claret- and blue- colored lingerie, the colors of Russell's beloved football team, West Ham United. In an added twist, Russell's nickname, "Rusty," was inscribed on the back of her panties. Russell tweeted: "Wow. Now MY GIRLFRIEND has worn a West Ham basque while hosting the EMAs. What a day! I might revive Gandhi and ask if he wants to be mates."

The two were getting closer. In an interview with *The Sunday Times*, Russell stated that his girlfriend was "lovely" and that he was looking forward to monogamy. He said: "I am living in a different way at the moment, regardless of what happens in my current situation. I am unlikely to be satisfied with the calamitous promiscuity of the preceding five or six years."

Even though it had only been a couple of months, their relationship took a serious turn when Katy introduced her boyfriend to her parents while they were in Austria. Russell, in fact, was already hinting at marriage. In an interview with *GMTV* in the United Kingdom he said: "It was a deep craving within me—I mistook it for lust. I thought I was promiscuous, but it turns out I was just thorough to get the right one. I'm ever so happy."

For the New Year, the pair jetted off to India and, on New Year's Eve, while at a tiger sanctuary in Rajasthan, Russell proposed and . . . Katy said yes. It seemed Katy had tamed her own tiger.

Lovebirds Katy Perry and Russell Brand at the 2010 Grammy Awards.

Grammy return

At the start of 2010, Katy was nominated for yet another Grammy Award. This time the accolade was for Best Female Pop Vocal Performance, thanks to the success of her big hit "Hot N Cold" from her June 2008 album *One of the Boys*.

Her competition was, of course, world-class, as she was up against Beyoncé for "Halo," Adele for "Hometown Glory," Pink for "Sober," and Taylor Swift for "You Belong with Me." Though Katy was only up for one Grammy—compared to Beyoncé's ten—she continued to attract the spotlight, whether she won or not. As Katy said: "It's crazy—all of a sudden, you're invited to all these fancy things. The people that wouldn't let you into this place or didn't want you coming there are now your best friends."

The Grammys—the Oscars of the music industry—are held annually by the National Academy of Recording Arts and Sciences. They are prized by recording artists around the globe. Even a nomination can change an artist's career, and the award is a huge accolade that recognizes outstanding achievement in the music industry. Katy was thrilled with her nomination and joked: "I think I can do this. I can maybe make a living. Maybe this is my job. Thanks, Grammys!"

As she arrived at the event, she couldn't contain her excitement as she sashayed down the red carpet. Known for her usually extravagant outfits, this time, Katy wore a nude gold-sequined backless dress by Zac Posen, Casadei heels, earrings by Dijan from Lebanon, and a Judith Leiber Elephant bag. "You never know who the winner is," said Katy. "It keeps you on your toes, so you dress to win. Which I always do, but I haven't won yet."

It was her second Grammy nomination after her nod for "I Kissed a Girl" in 2009—also for Best Female Pop Vocal Performance. As Katy chatted to journalists before the Grammys, she played down her excitement, joking about her second nomination: "Again? Jeez!" However, Katy quickly got serious, saying: "No, it wasn't that. It was, 'Thanks!' It was encouraging."

It was more than encouraging for Katy—it was proof that she had been accepted by her peers and that her work continued to be current and worthy of recognition. This was just the encouragement she needed before heading back into the recording studio to start work on her new album.

"I just started my new record," said Katy, "and to think that this little record [*One of the Boys*] that I [shed] blood, sweat and tears over for five years of making it and then being on the road for two years . . . it's been such a process. But to think it's still continuing is encouraging."

It was an exciting time in Katy's life and career. By now, she was a seasoned performer, with a world tour under her belt and several award trophies weighing down her

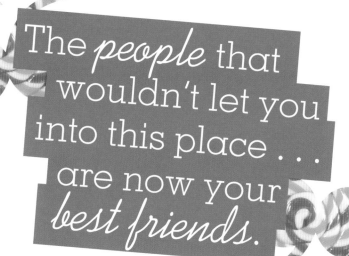

The *people* that wouldn't let you into this place . . . are now your *best friends*.

bookshelves. She was also attending the 2010 Grammys with a new prize on her arm—fiancé Russell Brand, known as one of the world's most notorious womanizers.

Katy had been asked to present the nominees for Best Rock Performance by a Duo or Group with Vocals, which went to Kings of Leon. Sadly, once again, it wasn't Katy's night. Katy's friend, Taylor Swift, and Beyoncé led the way. Beyoncé racked up six trophies—the most ever for a female artist on a single Grammy night—winning Best Female Pop Vocal Performance for "Halo." Taylor took home the show's biggest honor, nabbing Album of the Year for 2009's best-selling *Fearless*.

After the Grammys, Katy tweeted, "Tonight was lovely, don't think I'll be sleepin on 2010, it's time to show them aces eh! Goodnight everyone :)"

California Gurls

In 2009, Jay-Z's song "Empire State of Mind," an anthem celebrating New York City, had been the song of the year, with everyone from New York to Los Angeles singing along. Katy, a California native, decided the time had come for her home state to get a shout-out.

"I was hearing about that Jay-Z and Alicia Keys' song, 'Empire State of Mind' so much in California and I was jealous!" said Katy. "What about California? . . . What about the Beach Boys? Or Tupac? So I thought it would be time for a West Coast anthem with my twist."

"It's so great that 'Empire State of Mind' is huge and that everyone has the New York song, but what the f**k? What about LA? What about California?"

Katy admitted that she used Wikipedia to select a rapper to feature on the track. She knew she wanted a relevant hip-hop star and, after some online research, she decided on someone. It was, of course, "tha Doggfather."

The next stage was getting Snoop Dogg involved. Snoop is an iconic West Coast rapper, but would he want to work with Katy, a pop princess? Katy's plan involved flattery—she started writing the lyrics and included references to the hip-hop artist. Plus, he too was a California native.

"I went into the studio, brought the idea, and collaborated with some songwriters," said Katy. "And I started to insert obvious Snoop Dogg references like 'sipping gin and juice' and more obvious ones like 'Snoop Doggy Dogg on the stereo.' And I was like, 'If Snoop Dogg was on a song about the West Coast, it would be truly legit!' So I kind of lured him with all those little odes to Snoop Dogg already in the 'California Gurls' lyrics. He was so cool! He's like, chill."

Snoop Dogg was swift to return his admiration. He said in an interview that he collaborated with Katy "because she's a bad bitch, but she needed a gangster to complete the deal." He went on to tell the world that he was a fan of Katy's work, admiring her attitude, but he also insisted that it was his input on "California Gurls" that was key to the song's success.

Snoop stated: "She had a cake with no candles on it, then she put me on 'California Gurls,' and it went to number one. . . . I'm probably the most popular rapper in the world, but I don't make pop music. I make gangsta s**t. I don't cross over to pop—pop crosses over to me. . . . I don't ever aim for radio play. I make s**t that feels good to me, and if top forty radio catches wind, then great. If they don't, I'm still gonna do what I gotta do."

"California Gurls" was, of course, a huge hit—even before it was officially released. The song was somehow leaked online, so Capitol Records decided to release it early, moving the radio date forward two weeks to May 7, 2010. The song went on to stay at the top of the Billboard Hot 100 for six consecutive weeks, giving her a second U.S. number one single and Snoop Dogg his third. It reached number one in more than ten countries, including Australia, Canada, Ireland, New Zealand, and the United Kingdom. On December 2, 2010, the song received a Grammy nomination for Best Pop Collaboration with Vocals.

The accolades and popularity of the song continued as it became the first song to top the 300,000 mark in weekly digital sales more than once in 2010, with 318,000 and 359,000 copies sold in the first and second weeks of June, respectively. Within seven weeks of its release, "California Gurls" had sold more than two million downloads, which is the second-fastest pace in digital history behind Flo Rida's "Right Round."

Naturally, there were naysayers trying to create a scandal about the song and rumors abounded that the Beach Boys wanted to sue her for using the "California Girls" theme, something they had made famous nearly forty-five years earlier. However, Beach Boy cofounder Brian Wilson, who cowrote the original "California Girls" said: "I love her vocal. . . . She sounds very clear and energetic. The melody is infectious, and I'm flattered that Snoop Dogg used our lyric on the tag. I wish them well with this cut." With or without Brian's good wishes, the song has sold more than 5 million digital copies in the U.S. alone.

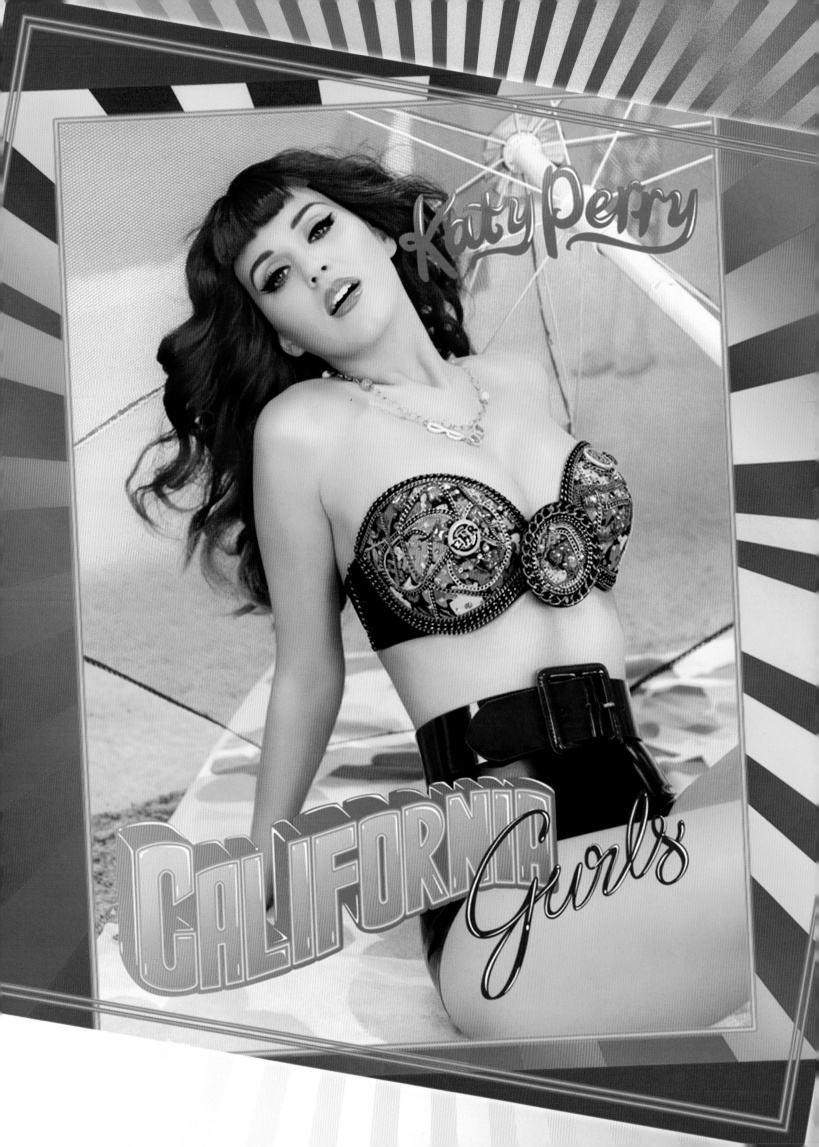

"I don't follow trends. I'm just not into what everyone else is wearing. I have my own look, which I call 'Lolita Meets Old Hollywood Glam.' But there are certain times when I want to mix it up and be edgier. For last New Year's Eve, for example, I looked S&M in this all-black corset dress from Dolce & Gabbana, lace tights, and five-inch heels."

Teenage Dream

With the award season behind her, it was time for Katy to head back into the studio. The pressure was on again to create a successful follow-up to *One of the Boys*. The key? Not wanting to abandon a winning formula, Katy reunited with her hit makers, former collaborators Dr. Luke and Max Martin, who took a more commanding role on this album. "I wanted to come back and work with them even more on this record," said Katy, "so instead of it being two songs we have six or seven on this record now."

For inspiration, Katy headed back to her hometown of Santa Barbara, California, to write the title track for *Teenage Dream*. "Going to Santa Barbara, which isn't very far from L.A., it was just like it brought me back home and it took me out of this fast-paced L.A.," Katy told MTV News. "Everybody climbing on top of each other to get to that next step on the ladder . . . sometimes L.A. can get exhausting."

"Teenage Dream" was that song that dictated how the entire album would play out. "I wrote that song in Santa Barbara and it was a really pure moment for me because that's where I'm from. And it was where I started my creative juices, and it kind of exudes this euphoric feeling like everyone remembers what their teenage dreams were," she said.

Katy had started recording the album in October 2009, and, when asked to comment on how the album was coming along, she said: "I'm heading to Las Vegas to hook up with The Dream and Tricky Stewart, who wrote 'Single Ladies' [for Beyoncé] and 'Umbrella' for Rihanna. It will be interesting to mash it up together to hopefully find an amazing new happy medium. My album is very premature, it's in the beginning stages but it's exciting to be back in the studio again."

In between tour dates, Katy was in and out of the studio for the next few months, and each time she left the studio, she would get more and more excited. She was maturing, and this new album was a reflection of who Katy was becoming. "*Teenage Dream* is a perfect snapshot into who I am in general—as a young woman, with my perspectives, convictions, anthems, and mottos. And it's kinda like *One of the Boys*. Maybe it's less cute and more sexy. It's full of different dimensions. It has songs like "California Gurls" that are really fun and obvious and then there are songs like "Firework" that would hopefully motivate you and make you want to move and there are songs like "Not Like the Movies," which is a love song. If you want to know about me, it's definitely the CD to get."

Always thinking ahead, Katy wanted the album to have more tempo in order to spice up her live shows. "Katy definitely knows what she wants and doesn't want. She has an amazing voice, great taste and she makes great videos. It's nice to work with an artist who can deliver your music so well," said Dr. Luke in an interview with *Billboard*. Dr. Luke, of course, was an instrumental part of the album, with credits on five songs, including "California Gurls," "Teenage Dream," and "E.T."

New collaborators on *Teenage Dream* included Stargate, a Norwegian record-producing duo and songwriting team, and Christopher "Tricky" Stewart, a seasoned music industry renaissance man. Tricky told *Rap-Up* magazine in December 2009 that the sound of the album would be pop and rock, like *One of the Boys*, though calling it a "different gear" for himself.

Even when working with all these superstar producers and songwriters, Perry said she stood her ground creatively from start to finish. "I'm in the studio fighting with them to change the melody, or I'm fighting for the best lyric at all times," she says. "I think we rewrote *Teenage Dream* five times for ten days straight. On the last day, I was so happy to finally get somewhere that we all agreed on."

The album was released on August 24, 2010, debuting at number one on the *Billboard* 200, selling 192,000 copies in its first week. It was later certified platinum two times by the Recording Industry Association of America (RIAA), selling more than 2 million copies in the United States and going on to sell approximately 5.5 million copies worldwide. It is also the only album ever to have seven songs top the *Billboard* Hot Dance Club Songs chart and the second album to have five of its singles peak at number one on the *Billboard* Hot 100 and the third. *Teenage Dream* was another incredible success for Katy Perry.

Close Sesame

Following the release of *Teenage Dream*, it was time for the promotional round of interviews, photo shoots, and television appearances. One such television show was the popular children's series *Sesame Street*.

Sesame Street is an institution in the United States, with just about every child across America having watched the antics of Big Bird, Oscar the Grouch, Count von Count, Elmo, and Bert and Ernie.

Sesame Street often features celebrities and, over the years, has included guest stars such as rock singers Alice Cooper and Gene Simmons of KISS; *Sopranos* actor James Gandolfini; and rapper Ice-T. In 2010, guests on the show included Ryan Reynolds, Jennifer Garner, and Jason Bateman. With the show having been on television for more than forty years, other famous stars on the show have included Lauren Bacall, Tony Bennett, Ray Charles, Ben Stiller, and James Earl Jones, as well as political figures such as Hilary Clinton, Michelle Obama, and Nancy Bush. So, when *Sesame Street* approached Katy's team, there was no way they were going to turn it down.

Katy's segment was due to feature her singing a version of "Hot N Cold" with Elmo, and she couldn't have been more excited. She turned up to the recording wearing a yellow-green Giles Deacon minidress, which featured a see-through mesh top and strapless sweetheart bustline.

The skit shows Katy asking Elmo to play dress up. Elmo can't decide whether to say yes or no and runs away, so Katy chases after the *Sesame Street* regular singing "Hot N Cold" to tease him about his indecisiveness over their playdate.

After the recording, Katy said that the duet with Elmo had been "the highlight of my entire career." She added: "I think some of these songs, even though sometimes they have a naughty dimension to them, they are so pop infectious it gets into kids . . . I love

that 'Hot N Cold' could translate to *Sesame Street*. I'm gonna have kids someday, and I love that some pop star out there is gonna change their lyrics to make my kids bounce in their diapers."

The segment was scheduled to air on New Year's Eve, but when the clip of Katy's guest spot hit the Internet, the scandal over it started to kick off. With the clip getting more than one million hits on YouTube, parents across America were complaining about Katy's revealing costume.

Public Broadcast Service (PBS), which airs *Sesame Street*, received so many complaints they, together with *Sesame Street* producers, decided to pull the segment. In fact, the producers issued an official statement: "In light of the feedback we've received on the Katy Perry music video which was released on YouTube only, we have decided we will not air the segment on the television broadcast of *Sesame Street*, which is aimed at preschoolers."

Carol-Lynn Parente, the show's producer, said on *Good Morning America*: "We would never, never produce anything that we thought was inappropriate. We were surprised not only by the amount of feedback but how fast it came in. It was a lot . . . We have a great interactive relationship with our viewers, particularly parents. They trust *Sesame Street*. We take that seriously, and so we viewed a lot of the feedback and made what we thought was an appropriate decision."

Appearing alongside Parente, Elmo himself said he's not done with Katy yet. "Elmo loves Ms. Katy and we had a good time. So we'll have another date," he said, popping up from behind the anchor couch. "Yes, yes, Ms. Katy. Come, come, come, come, we'll have another playdate!"

Later that year, Katy found humor in the incident when she was hosting *Saturday Night Live* and parodied the incident. Furthermore, it also earned her a guest spot on one of the world's most popular cartoon shows, *The Simpsons*.

Katy appeared to relish the scandal Eager to get viewers to log on to her *Sesame* moment; she tweeted: "Wow, looks like my playdate with Elmo has been cut short! If you still wanna play see it at www.katyperry.com Tag you're it, Elmo!" As yet, Elmo is still waiting for his new playdate with Ms. Katy.

CARMEN MIRANDA

Ever wondered how Katy comes up with her crazy stage outfits and sets and why there seems to be so much fruit involved? In the 1940s, a Brazilian samba singer dominated Hollywood. Portuguese-born, her name was Carmen Miranda and, at the time, she was widely reported to be one of the highest-earning women in the U.S. She was the star of many films, including *The Gang's All Here* in 1943 and *Doll Face* in 1946. She continued to be hugely succesful until her death in 1955. Her signature style, including fruit-laden hats, turbans, and jewelry, and platform sandals is still immediately recognizable around the world and has influenced many fashion designers over the years. Carmen Miranda is also one of Katy Perry's heroes, a huge influence on her style choices and stage designs.

When Katy arrived in Rio for the "Rock in Rio" event in September 2011, she teased photographers eager to catch a glimpse of the rock princess by arriving masked. Her mask of choice? The legendary Carmen Miranda, complete with a signature fruit hat. Katy walked through the airport with a companion sporting an identical mask—the pair channelled Carmen as they made their way to the waiting car.

This wasn't the first time Katy had paid tribute to the influential movie star. Back in 2009, when performing at the Grammys, she wore a Carmen Miranda-style dress, designed by The Blonds, decorated with fake bananas, grapes, and strawberries.

Katy, like her icon, loves fruit. Whether it's fruity clothing or blow-up bananas, it is a recurring theme at her performances. This is a girl who loves a cherry chapstick, has been photographed wearing sparkling bustiers bursting with strawberries and a seed-studded watermelon romper suit when performing on the *Today* show in 2008. She also emerged from a giant banana peel at the KIIS FM Jingle Ball that same year. And then there is the accessorizing—the strawberry hairpins, watermelon earrings, fruit-charm bracelets, even sequined banana gloves.

Julie Mollo, a designer from Massachusetts, was the creator of a white romper suit featuring sequined banana peels and banana-inspired gloves that Katy wore to the MTV VMAs in 2008. "When I was first sketching for Katy Perry," said Mollo, "I knew she liked fruit, so I gave her fruit. I was inspired by a banana. I am not subtle, gentle, or discreet by any means."

Katy Perry is not known for her subtlety or discretion either. When she likes a style, she lets the world know. In 2009, on the Hello Katy Tour, she said: "I have the guy who creates stages for Madonna working on this tour. I'm indulging my obsession with fruit and cats and designing all different outfits."

It isn't just Katy's outfits that have been inspired by this fruit fixation. While on tour, her stage has occasionally been decorated with giant inflatable fruit. "It started with my obsession with the 1940s and cherry charm bracelets and strawberry-and-cherry pattern baskets on women's dresses," she explained. "Then my obsession got really big when I went to Japan and I'd see dancing bananas with faces on them. So I decided to take it to a whole other level. It's fun, it's kitsch, it's cute. Some of it is phallic. Some of it is playful. I have no idea."

Of course, with such strong fashion and style ideas, Katy has said she'd like to develop a clothing line based on her bizarre fashion sense, but is currently too busy with her music to devote the time to fashion. "It would take two years to do it right," Katy says. "I don't want to do something rushed and sloppy. I look at something like Gwen Stefani's line, L.A.M.B., and that took forever to do."

Who knows—in a few years' time, fruit hats may yet be worn by every little girl across the globe as the spirit of Carmen Miranda comes alive thanks to the dreams of a young girl called Katy from Santa Barbara.

KATY CHANNELS CARMEN MIRANDA AT THE 2009 GRAMMYS, AND MIRANDA HERSELF.

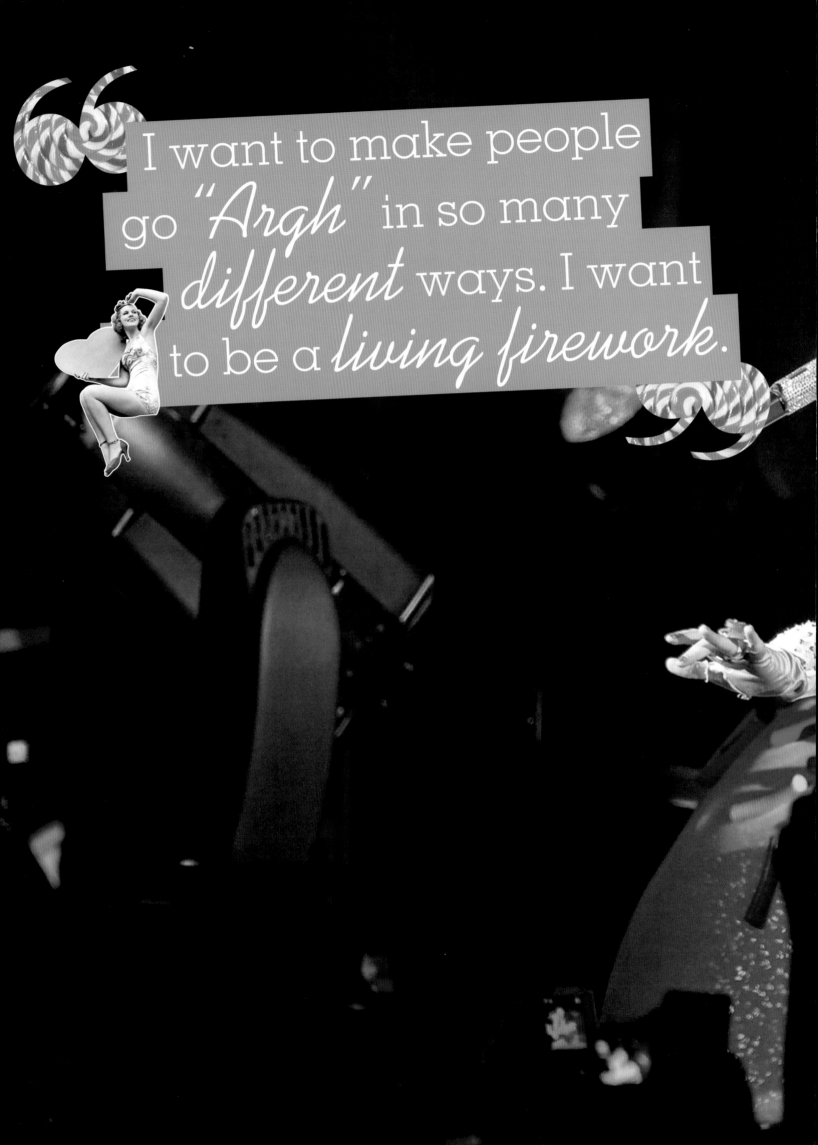

"I want to make people go "Argh" in so many different ways. I want to be a living firework.

Explosive times

Katy's favorite song on *Teenage Dream* was "Firework." So, when she set out planning the video for it, she wanted it to be perfect. She managed to snag Dave Meyers, one of the world's leading music video directors, who had previously worked with Pink, Kelly Clarkson, and T.I.

"'Firework' is probably my favorite song on the record because it really shows who I am now and the message I want to send to people in a way and hopefully it's an encouraging one. And to me, I've always been on the lookout for a song to really uplift me but wasn't so cheesy. 'Firework' is like an anthem, and also it talks about making people go 'aah' and I wanna make people go 'aah.'"

The inspiration for the song came from Jack Kerouac's *On the Road*. Russell, a big Kerouac fan, told Katy about a passage in the book that resonated with Katy: "It was a paragraph that he said I was like," she says. "In the book he was talking about how he wanted to be around people who were buzzing, fizzing and making people go 'Argh, like fireworks across the sky.' I guess that's my whole vibe. I want to make people go 'Argh' in so many different ways. I want to be a living firework. . . . Sometimes you're in a situation where it feels like this is the best you can get. I really do believe in true love and you should really find it."

Katy worked on the song with a number of other writers—Mikkel S. Eriksen, Tor Erik Hermansen, Sandy Wilhelm, and Ester Dean—and was excited about shooting her video in Budapest with Dave Meyers. The feeling was mutual.

Dave said that he was looking to "play with [her] image a bit . . . sort of demystify the candy-colored pop icon that she's become. . . . We wanted to articulate the meaning of that song: what it means to be an underdog and have the courage, if you're on the outskirts of society, to be your own person," he said.

Katy's team put out an open casting call so that her fans could have the opportunity to take part in the video, and they were overwhelmed when more than 38,000 people responded. The initial concept of the shoot was kept a secret, but Katy, once again, used Twitter to keep her fans informed and thank them all for working so hard. Katy tweeted: "Not gonna stop shooting till the sun comes up cause we are a LIGHT in a dark place!" She wrapped the shoot on September 30, saying, "I want to thank all the magical people that brought their sparks to this video the past few days . . . your light reminded me of my purpose."

"I had written the treatment already with the idea of deconstructing her a little bit, and then 'Teenage Dream' came out and deconstructed her all the way," Meyers said. "So I had to switch gears a little bit. But really, it was easy, because I connected with the song. I felt 'Firework' was very personal, and I was very drawn to that."

In October, just days before the release of "Firework," Katy decided to dedicate the video to the It Gets Better campaign, a project founded in September 2010 to help prevent the growing number of suicides among lesbian, gay, bisexual, and transgender teenagers. Ultimately—like Christina Aguilera's "Beautiful"—the song has become an anthem for people who had battled bullies or struggled to find themselves.

"I think that's why I wrote it, because I really believe in people and I believe that people have a spark to be a firework," Katy said. "It's just up to them, and a lot of times it's only us that's standing in the way of reaching our goals, fulfilling our destinies, being the best version of who we possibly can be, so that's why I wrote it."

In the United States, "Firework" reached number one on the *Billboard* Hot 100. By this time she was the first female artist since Monica in 1998–99 to have three consecutive singles from an album top the chart. By January 2011, "Firework" had sold 509,000 digital downloads in the United States, the second highest number sold by a female artist. It is one of three Katy Perry songs to top 5 million paid downloads—the others being "Hot N Cold" and "California Gurls"—making her the first artist in digital history to sell 5 million or more copies of three different hits.

"I never want to be boring, so therefore I aspire to always be interesting, experimental and entertaining. There are many cards in my deck of personality."

Sweet smell of success

A true mark of success these days can be measured by a scent—a celebrity scent—with pop stars such as Beyoncé, Justin Bieber, Britney Spears, Christina Aguilera, Kylie Minogue, Mariah Carey, and Celine Dion all having launched their own perfumes. In November 2010, it was Katy's turn. Her global popularity and marketability was translating into products for her fans and, first on the list—a perfume!

The fragrance was called "Purr," thanks to Katy's well-publicized love of cats. After all, Katy's mascot was her own cat Kitty Purry, who had even made a cameo in the "I Kissed a Girl" video. Also, during Katy's shows on her Hello Katy Tour, Katy always had a large inflatable Kitty Purry head onstage for decoration. So it was only natural that her perfume incorporate a cat.

The project was a joint venture with Gigantic Parfums, and Katy was deeply involved in the development of her signature scent—after all, this was, essentially, *eau de Katy*. After spending time with the experts, she finally approved of a scent she felt was worthy enough to carry the "Purr" name and the "Katy Perry" brand.

Working with Firmenich, Katy was aiming for a fragrance with a pronounced effect, one that stood apart from others already on the market. According to Nordstrom National Beauty and Fragrance Director Cheri Botiz, Perry was working alongside perfumers to "capture the distinctive notes of her favorite perfumes."

The Nordstrom director issued a further statement: "We are excited to partner with Katy Perry and Gigantic Parfums as the exclusive retailer for Purr. The sophisticated, playful energy of the fragrance makes it a must-have for the holiday season and beyond."

Naturally, Katy was delighted about the launch of her perfume: "I'm absolutely thrilled to finally introduce me in a bottle," said Katy. "There is a wonderful world of fragrances out there, but like with my music, I believe there is room for me and my own unique twist on it. Purr is a natural extension of who I am as a woman—it's a gorgeous blend of all my favorite scents that embodies my style, my tastes, and my love for all things incredibly cute. It is an absolutely purrfect perfume that I hope leaves you meowing with delight!"

Katy insisted on having a hands-on approach. It wasn't just the smell that she was involved in, but also the packaging and design of the bottle. Naturally, the cat theme continued—after all, this was a woman who has appeared on stage as Catwoman, alongside an oversized blow-up cat. With that kind of feline affinity, it was no surprise that Katy created a lavender cat-shaped bottle complete with jeweled eyes and metallic accents.

By November of 2010, the perfume was ready to be launched. But would it sell? This was a huge gamble for Katy and her team—what if it failed? What if no one bought the product? The headlines of her "sweet smell of failure" might damage the Katy Perry brand which, at that point, was incredibly strong and successful. As it turned out, no one could have foreseen the phenomenal success of Purr.

When Katy launched the product in London, thousands gathered at Selfridges department store on Oxford Street, creating pandemonium as they struggled to catch a glimpse of Katy, who spent several hours greeting fans and personally signing perfume boxes for the first hundred customers. The Purr party continued. And, such was Katy's popularity that Purr became the best-selling fragrance for the first nine weeks of its release. As Katy said: "It's been out for nine weeks and it's been number one for nine weeks"—a phenomenal debut. Once again, Katy had triumphed!

Katy promoting her first perfume, Purr.

Here comes the bride

In October 2010, Katy should have been preparing for one of the biggest days in any woman's life—her wedding. However, when you're Katy Perry, there's rarely any downtime to relax or have a personal life, let alone plan a wedding! She had just finished shooting her "Firework" video, buying a place in New York (for a cool $2.75 million), touring in Eastern Europe, and promoting her latest album. Apparently, it was her fiancé who was putting in the hours planning the wedding.

Katy even commented on how, due to her packed schedule, it was Russell, who was concerned with making plans for their upcoming nuptials. "He's a total bridezilla," joked Katy. "He's like a freak, man. . . . You should see—he's always, like, buying bride magazines. Every time we go out for breakfast he's like, 'Can we just stop and get a bride magazine?'"

The couple had gotten engaged on New Year's Eve in 2009, and it was only nine months later that they were planning on walking up the aisle. That might seem quick to most people, but, at the time, Katy truly felt that he was the one, and the feeling was mutual. Katy said: "I always knew I wanted a great man of God, someone who was going to be an inspiration for people and also be a lovely husband and father. We're at different places in our lives, but we can still grow together. He's thought-provoking, articulate, a real advocate. I also definitely wanted to have a laugh. I have all that in him."

By October 20, 2010, a few days before Katy's twenty-sixth birthday, the couple arrived in India for their wedding. As all their movements were played out in the media, it was natural for Katy to use her Twitter account to let the world know that they wanted privacy. Just after they arrived in Jaipur, India, Katy wrote: "I have something to say . . . TWIT BREAK: Greatest gift u can give us is respect & [love]

during this private X. No use wasting ur X w/ STOLEN or FALSE info. Thnk u for this."

A week earlier, Russell had conducted an interview with the MTV show *The Seven* in which he had made his love for Katy clear, saying, "Marriage takes place in the heart. So in that sense, we are already married."

The media speculation continued, especially after friends and relatives—Katy's father and siblings (David and Angela) along with Russell's mother Barbara—were spotted arriving in Jaipur. Russell and Katy even went as far as hiring a "decoy couple," who were spotted at the airport with Katy's stylist, Logan Horne, Russell's manager (and reported best man), Nik Linnen, and Katy's friend, Markus Molinari. In total, around eighty of the pair's closest friends and family attended.

On the Friday before the wedding, the pair hosted a Bollywood-themed party for all of their friends. Russell wore a traditional Indian ensemble of loose informal trousers and a long baggy tunic in white, while Katy rocked a plain red sari. As they arrived at the venue, they were greeted by acrobats and jugglers, and the pair partied away.

At around five in the evening on Saturday, October 23, Katy walked down the aisle in an Elie Saab haute couture dress in dove gray with lace sleeves. The location was a wildlife sanctuary at Ranthambore, a stunning venue renowned for its tigers and located 150 miles southeast of Jaipur. The pair embraced traditional Indian rituals, with music provided by instruments such as the sitar, the santoor, the tabla, and kettledrums, as well as Rajasthani folk music.

The next day, the pair tweeted matching messages, saying: "We did!" with an accompanying photo of signs on a wall that read "Katy" and "Russell." With the world watching, the pair issued a statement confirming their marriage: "The very private and spiritual ceremony, attended by the couples' closest family and friends, was performed by a Christian minister and longtime friend of the Hudson Family. The backdrop was the inspirational and majestic countryside of northern India." Sadly, no one could have guessed how quickly the fairy-tale wedding was going to come to an end . . . because, at this point, everything seemed perfect, and Katy and Russell couldn't have been more in love.

Katy

Russell

I'm always thinking. My **BRAIN** never turns off. I keep a **NOTEBOOK** with me to write down headlines that I see in my **TRAVELS** and have a voice recorder for quick **MELODIES** that pop into my head. I started to think about people I would love to work with on the next **RECORD** . Some of them probably would not have taken my **CALL** last year. But, I am still caught in the wonderful hurricane that is **MY FIRST RECORD!**

CALIFORNIA

Dreams

The end of 2010 brought Katy more incredible news—she was nominated for the Grammys again. This time for four awards, including Album of the Year for *Teenage Dream*.

Katy was up against some of the most acclaimed artists of the day, including Beyoncé and Eminem. Her other nominations included Best Female Pop Vocal Performance for "Teenage Dream," Best Pop Collaboration with Vocals for "California Gurls," and Best Pop Vocal Album.

Katy was handpicked to open *Grammy Nominations Concert Live!*—the live television concert—with her global hit "California Gurls." Wearing a glittery silver minidress covered in snowflake details, Katy gave a rousing rendition of the song.

The list of nominations seemed to catch Katy by surprise, so much so that she blasphemed on the live telecast of the *Grammy Nominations Concert Live!* When LL Cool J picked her out in the audience, giving her a shout-out: "Are you feeling some Grammy love tonight?" Katy replied: "Hell, yes!" For Katy, with her religious background, this was huge. Quickly looking somewhat abashed, she issued an immediate apology, holding her hands together as if in prayer. After the ceremony, Katy tweeted the simple message "#GOD."

Katy was floating on air. Four nominations was a big deal for the California native, especially considering where she came from. Rejected by various record labels and a debut album that sold two hundred copies—but here she was . . . a four-time Grammy nominated artist. "It's exciting, I'm really happy!" Katy said. "I called my hubby and he said, 'Well done!' This year seems like it's going to be a big year and [it's] a nice way to finish the year too . . . I am so blessed."

Katy was also asked to perform at the Grammys ceremony, so she had to decide which songs to pick from her nominated *Teenage Dream* album. "I am very excited about that. It is going to be an amazing performance," said Katy. "I can say it is a medley of songs from the record and there will be little surprises here and there."

Katy and Russell seemed to love using Twitter as a medium to connect with their fans and, the next morning, Valentine's Day, which was also the day of the Grammys, Katy was back on Twitter: "& thank u to all the AMAZING #TEAMKATY people I've been blessed to surround myself with . . . couldn't do it w/out u. It takes a village!"

Katy had brought two guests to the party, her husband Russell Brand and Ann Hudson, her grandmother, who was celebrating her ninetieth birthday.

"If I don't go home with any Grammys, I still go home with my Grammy," joked Katy to Ryan Seacrest as he interviewed her on the red carpet. Katy's gift to her "Grammy" was a bedazzled walking cane. Katy felt "amazing" to be nominated and recognized by fellow musicians. "You feel popular, I guess," she said.

It was a busy night for Katy. When she wasn't racing backstage for an outfit change, she was either performing or nervously listening to see if her name was announced. Was it going to be third time lucky for Mrs. Brand?

For her onstage performance of "Not Like the Movies," Katy dangled on a swing in another Armani creation. She was hoisted up into the air and sang about love and finding the perfect man. Not only was it Grammy night, but it was also Katy and Russell's first Valentine's Day together as husband and wife. Footage of their wedding was the backdrop to the performance— the first time the couple had released any images of their special day.

In the end, although Katy didn't pick up any awards, she had something more that night. She had the support and love of her husband and grandmother. It was a night to remember.

Katy performing "Teenage Dream" at the Grammy Awards, February 13, 2011, in Los Angeles.

Dream tour

With her Valentine's Day Grammy performance behind her, it was time for Katy to pack her bags and say good-bye to her husband of four months. She had to prepare for her grueling California Dreams tour, which was due to kick off on February 20, 2011, and last until January 22, 2012.

"It's like training for the Olympics. I'm off to the gym to build stamina . . . and I hate working out, but I have to go, because this is a really energetic show," Katy said. "It's not like I'm going to make my fortune off touring; I'm basically doing this as a big IOU for all the love and support I've gotten. I need to go shake some hands and kiss some people."

This was Katy's second concert tour to support *Teenage Dream*, and the plan was ambitious—Katy was going to spend twelve months touring Europe, Australia, Asia, and the Americas. As for "not making her fortune off touring," Katy did pretty well. Ultimately, she played 124 shows, and the tour earned more than $59 million.

As ever, Katy used Twitter to let her fans know about plans for the show: "[Opening act] @robynkonichiwa [Robyn] and I will be dancing up a storm watching your set! Can't wait, BTE! . . . best tour ever!" she wrote. "I feel like this tour is building a bridge between the hipsters & the popsters. Hip-Pop is so 2011. Get wit it. #californiadreamstour!"

Of course, Katy had big plans for the show. She was growing as an artist, loved being a performer, and wanted to make sure her fans were treated to a spectacle. "I'm definitely bringing the pizzazz with a lot of bells and whistles," said Katy, speaking to her fans. "I hope that it's going to engage all of your senses: sight, sound, smell, taste, touch. I'm really excited about incorporating the look and the idea of some of the songs on tour and making a massive production of it," she said. "I'm gonna want a lot of visuals. I want it to be ten times better than when I was on tour last."

In order to "raise the bar" and bring in the "pizzazz," Katy hired Pink's touring director, and she even had a few tricks to make her show as original as possible—she added "Smell-O-Vision" to the mix!

"It's the first concert that's going to smell good," Katy said. "It's going to smell like you're in cotton candy heaven. It's a fun little nuance. I am a woman of detail, and you will be seeing that—even down to the fifteen outfit changes I'm doing in concert."

The tour kicked off in Lisbon, Portugal, where she paid tribute to her friend Rihanna by performing an acoustic medley of "Only Girl (In the World)" before covering a few more chart-topping hits, such as Jay-Z's song "Big Pimpin'" and Willow Smith's "Whip My Hair." The crowd went crazy—once again Katy had another successful tour on her hands.

The next few weeks were a blur for Katy. From Lisbon she went to Milan, then Zurich, Munich, Vienna, Berlin, Offenbach, Paris, Brussels, Cologne, Hamburg, and Amsterdam before, one month later, arriving in London. By now, Katy was heading up a sell-out tour, which she still couldn't believe. As she said: "To say that you had a sold-out arena tour, in the first five years of your career . . . it's not supposed to happen like that."

After Katy wrapped the European leg of her tour, she headed off to sold-out shows in Australia, New Zealand, and Japan. The Katy Perry juggernaut was continuing its journey toward America, and the success proved to be phenomenal as her crew made sure she constantly surprised her plethora of fans.

"This tour is running for over a year," said concert director Baz Halpin. "So it's great that every time that it goes back to a new territory it's gotten bigger and it's different and there's new elements added, and it's Katy making sure that everybody gets a fresh perspective and fresh new show every time they go see it."

By the time the tour had finished at the end of January 2012, it was ranked sixteenth in Pollstar's "2011 Top 25 Worldwide Tours," earning more than $59.5 million. At the end of 2011—with another month on the road to cover—it had still ranked thirteenth on *Billboard*'s annual "Top 25 Tours," earning nearly $50 million with the first 98 shows. Katy Perry was truly a star—with a sold-out tour to prove it.

Katy Perry

THE **California Dreams** TOUR 2011

SATURDAY 05 NOVEMBER 2011
NOTTINGHAM TRENT
FM ARENA
0844 124 624 | 0844 871 8803 | kililive.com
the album 'teenage dream' out now   www.katyperry.com
A Kilimanjaro presentation in association with CAA

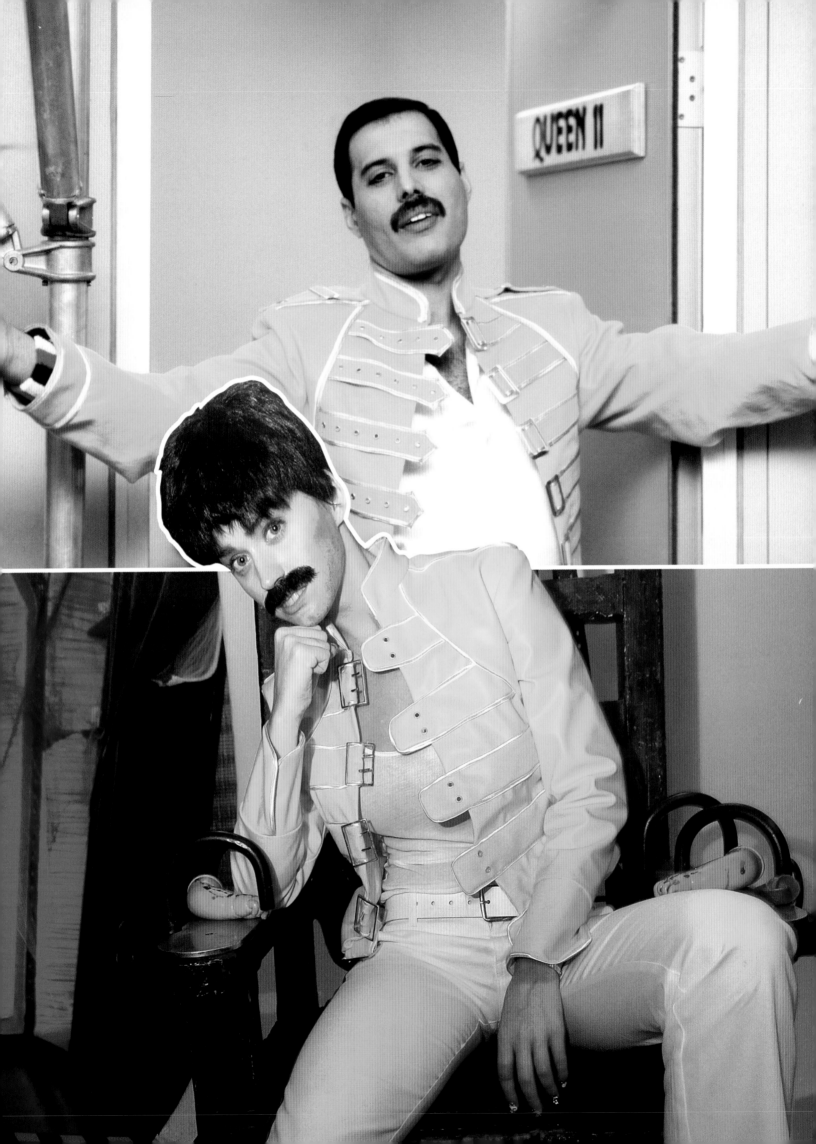

FREDDIE MERCURY

One of Katy's earliest influences was rock god Freddie Mercury, lead singer of the British band Queen. Freddie was born Farrokh Bulsara in Zanzibar in 1946. His family moved to London where Freddie met fellow band members Brian May, Roger Taylor, and Brian Deacon while studying at Imperial College, London. The band hit the big time in the 1970s with hits such as "Bohemian Rhapshody" and "Killer Queen." They went to become one of the biggest bands in the 1980s who could fill huge stadiums around the world. Freddie's performance at Live Aid in 1985 has become the stuff of legend. A flamboyant and openly gay artist, Freddie is often mentioned as being one of the best rock singers of all time. He may seem to some an unusual choice of icon for the young, sheltered Christian Katy Perry, but his voice, theatricality, and flamboyance drew her in and has influenced her ever since.

Katy has frequently expressed her adoration of Mercury: "Yeah. I'm a huge fan of Freddie Mercury. I'm a fan of lots of music, but he was a turning point. I wasn't allowed to listen to secular music when I was kid, but there was a time when I was hanging out at my friend's house. We're trying on all our outfits, like girls do, and out of nowhere I heard the lyrics to 'Killer Queen.' Time stood still. The music was totally different from anything I'd heard. I still love Freddie Mercury. He was flamboyant with a twist of the operatic, but more importantly he just didn't give a f***."

At the time, Katy was slowly moving away from the Gospel influences of her early childhood into the more mature choices of a teenager. When she heard "Killer Queen," everything stopped. "It was a moment where everything kind of went in slow motion. The clouds moved away, the sun started shining and I was like, 'I've found it! I've found an artist I want to be like! Everybody has that one person they want to be, that poster on the wall: Elvis, Madonna. For me it was a song called 'Killer Queen'—I wanted to be like Freddie Mercury."

In a statement to *NME*, Katy said, "Freddie Mercury was—and remains—my biggest influence. The combination of his sarcastic approach to writing lyrics and his 'I don't give a f***' attitude really inspired my music."

On what would have been Freddie Mercury's sixty-fifth birthday, a number of renowned rock artists got together to record tributes to the Queen frontman. Katy, of course, joined the tributes and sang "Happy Birthday" to her hero. Gazing at the camera, Katy said: "We love you, you're not really gone. You inspired me especially. Without you, I wouldn't be making music or doing what I do. Your lyrics inspired me as a fifteen-year-old girl. I heard 'Killer Queen' and I wanted to be a Killer Queen so thank you so much for all your amazing music."

Katy's love of Freddie is apparent to any of her fans. He's one of the few artists whose songs have repeatedly featured on her playlist over the years. In 2009, she sang "Don't Stop Me Now," and opened the MTV VMAs that year with "We Will Rock You" alongside Joe Perry. "Killer Queen" is frequently a part of her musical set.

Katy has always let the world know how much she admires Freddie. In 2011, she even dressed up like him in order to raise money for the late star's charity. Pictures of Katy wearing a mustache, cropped wig, and bright yellow jacket were broadcast across the world—Katy was promoting the "Freddie for a Day" campaign, which raised money for the AIDS charity The Mercury Phoenix Trust.

> "Time stood still. The music was totally different from anything I'd heard. I still love Freddie Mercury."

KATY PERRY DRESSED AS HER IDOL FREDDIE MERCURY AT HER TWENTY-FOURTH BIRTHDAY PARTY.

E.T. comes home

In a bid to keep her fans on their toes, it took Katy a while to decide which song to release next from *Teenage Dream*. With "Firework" still riding high in the charts, she asked her fans for their opinions. Initially it looked like "Peacock" was going to be her next single, but Katy kept all her fans guessing. "Thanks for all your great suggestions for the next single today!" she tweeted on December 13, 2010. "Your voice has been heard! We're on the same page. . . ." By February—just as Katy was launching her tour—a remix of "E.T." was released.

Katy reached out to her loyal fans by using her Facebook page to release the artwork for the single: "Here's a sneak peek of the artwork for 'E.T.,' the next single off *Teenage Dream*! Stay tuned for a new music video and remixes coming soon."

The track "E.T." wasn't even destined for Katy initially, but for another highly successful group, Three 6 Mafia—an Academy Award–winning rap group from Memphis, Tennessee.

"I remember writing with Max Martin and Dr. Luke," said Katy, "and there's this producer they wrote with, named Ammo, and they were just showing me different samples of songs or tracks or beats, and they accidentally pulled up this beat, and it was for Three 6 Mafia. I heard it and I always knew I wanted to write this futuristic, alienistic song, and they pulled it up and I was like, 'Wait, I can wrap my head around this. I know this seems like a long shot, but I think I have the perfect material to put on top of this sound.' And I did, and it really worked out perfectly."

It was certainly a different type of sound for Katy. By this point in 2011, Katy had been writing songs for more than ten years, so her style had naturally grown and matured—something that her fans definitely noticed and commented on. "It's interesting to see a lot of the commentary that goes along with growth," Katy said. "People are like, 'OK, I like her,' finally, or like, 'Damn, I hate to admit it, but we're on the

Katy Perry train,' which is really exciting, and I feel like I worked really hard for that."

"I knew starting with 'I Kissed a Girl' that it might have taken a little bit longer to get everybody onboard the Katy Perry train, I guess," she added. "But now, I'm having so much fun and I get to be so creative and try different things and expand, and I never play it safe—in any way, really."

The song definitely marked a departure for Katy even she commented that it was a "whole different vibe" for her with its "urban feel." Thanks to Katy's hard work and dedication, she was talented enough to be able to experiment successfully, despite the confusion of some of her fans. "People are so perplexed," said Katy, when talking about the video for "E.T." "They're like, 'Katy Perry, you're supposed to be Betty Boop! You're supposed to be wearing pink!' It's exciting to be able to push my audience, to be like, 'There's always more, I've got all of this hidden up my sleeve that I've really longed to show people."

The single marked another success for Katy. It reached number one in the United States, Canada, New Zealand, and Poland; and the top five in Australia, Ireland, and the United Kingdom.

When the single went to number one, Katy couldn't contain herself and tweeted at Kanye West—one of her coproducers on it, whose rap verses feature in the official version of the song—to let him know the news: "@kanyewest congrats friend, we did it! #sweet." "E.T." went on to set a record for the most weekly radio plays in the eighteen-year history of the chart. During the week of April 25 to May 1, 2011, Nielsen Broadcast Data Systems registered 12,330 plays over its 131 stations—an average of 94 plays per station, beating Katy's previous record with "California Gurls,". And this wasn't the only record Katy was going to break in 2011.

"I'm *competitive* with myself, and that goes hand in hand with how I *present* myself. I'm not only trying to put one foot in front of the other, I'm trying to put my *best foot forward.*"

Record Breaker

In 2011, 26-year-old Katy Perry celebrated another milestone. Despite her popular track "E.T." being knocked off the number one spot on the *Billboard* Hot 100 (by Grammy award–winning Adele's "Rolling in the Deep"), Katy's music had been in the Top 10 of the Hot 100 for a full 365 days.

Thanks to the success of the songs "California Gurls," "Teenage Dream," "Firework," and "E.T.," Katy's music had spent fifty-two consecutive weeks with a song at or near the top of the charts. No artist had ever spent an entire year in the Top 10—only Katy Perry. Even artists such as The Rolling Stones, the Beatles, and Elvis Presley are unable to claim a year of dominance—though, of course, the *Billboard* charts are very different these days.

The journey for Katy began when her hit song "California Gurls"—featuring a collaboration with Snoop Dogg—debuted at number two in May 2010. Such was the success of the song that it hit number one the following month and spent six weeks at the top of the chart before floating around the Top 10 for a while longer.

In July 2010, Katy released her next single from *Teenage Dream*, the title track. By September 2010, that too was number one, and there it stayed for two weeks. Though it dropped from the top spot, it continued to stick around the Top 10.

By November 2010, "Teenage Dream" was beginning to slip out of the Top 10, but luckily, her next release, "Firework"—released in October 2010—began its reign, spending four weeks at the top spot. So by the time "E.T." burst onto the scene in March 2011 and secured a top spot, Katy's domination of the chart was complete. There really was no one to match her.

Katy's appearance on the chart for an entire year bested the record of Swedish band Ace of Base, which had held the Hot 100's uninterrupted Top 10 run for forty eight straight weeks with "All That She Wants," "The Sign," and "Don't Turn Around" (1993 through 1994). Santana ranks third, with forty two consecutive weeks in the upper region (1999 through 2000), while Mariah Carey follows in fourth position with forty one weeks in a row (1995 through 1996).

It probably helped Katy's cause that, according to Nielsen Broadcast Data Systems, she was the most played artist on the radio during 2011. Ultimately, Katy clocked up 1,457,000 "detections" on U.S. radio that year, placing her slightly ahead of Bruno Mars with 1,440,000 plays. "E.T." was her most played song with 526,000 detections, followed by "Firework" with 509,000 plays, and "Last Friday Night (T.G.I.F.)," released in June 2011, with 450,000.

With sales of 1,451,000 since its August 2010 release, according to Nielsen SoundScan, *Teenage Dream* bested the sales of Perry's 2008 breakthrough album, *One of the Boys*, which has sold over 1,383,000. Even with a supportive label, accomplished and veteran publicists, and a team of music experts by her side, the phenomenon of Katy's consistency and ongoing popularity all comes down to her talent and ability as an artist.

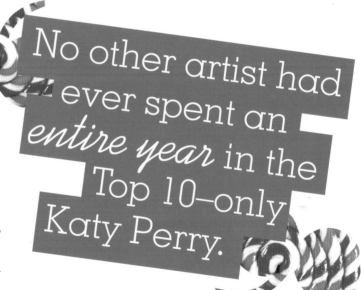

No other artist had ever spent an *entire year* in the Top 10—only Katy Perry.

By going on tour, she put herself in the spotlight, allowing herself to be held accountable to numerous critics all over the world. Singing live can often prove the undoing of many a seasoned artist—but not Katy Perry. Instead, her shows received rave reviews, and her music was bought by fans across the globe. Katy had proved herself to be a consistent artist, and, in a culture in which some people seek entertainment in the form of 140-word tweets, this was an incredible achievement, worthy of celebration.

Last Friday Night

On June 6, 2011, Katy was getting ready for the start of the North American leg of her California Dreaming tour. Excited fans were gathering in Duluth, just outside Atlanta, for the first concert as Katy rolled into town. On the same day, her latest single, "Last Friday Night (T.G.I.F.)" from her *Teenage Dream* album was officially released.

As the track soared up the charts, Katy traveled around the United States, working hard every night as she got up on stage to give her fans a concert to remember. Her set list, naturally, included the new single, as well as all the other number ones notched up over the previous year. The question on everyone's lips was—would this single make it to number one, too?

Katy was already in the record books in 2011. Thanks to the phenomenal success of her singles, Katy had spent more than a year in the Top 10. Upon its release, "Last Friday Night (T.G.I.F.)" also flew into the Top 10, joining her previous song "E.T.," which was still high in the charts.

It was an exciting time for Katy and her team. If "Last Friday Night (T.G.I.F.)" reached number one, Katy would be the first female artist to achieve five chart-topping songs from one album—and also the first artist of either sex to accomplish the feat since Michael Jackson had five number one hits from his *Bad* album in 1987 and 1988.

Although "Last Friday Night (T.G.I.F.)" was already doing incredibly well on the *Billboard* Digital Songs chart, Katy and her record company were hoping that it would be her sixth single to pass the four-million mark in digital sales, joining "E.T.," "California Gurls," and "Firework" from her *Teenage Dream* album, as well as "Hot N Cold" and "I Kissed a Girl" from *One of the Boys*. Until Katy, no other artist had ever had four songs pass the four-million downloads mark. Her closest competitors were Lady Gaga and Rihanna, who, as of June 2011, had each had three four-million sellers. By February 2012, the single passed the three million downloads mark in the United States alone.

The video for "Last Friday Night (T.G.I.F.)" features Katy dancing around as her alter ego, the dorky Kathy Beth Terry, who wears braces, headgear, and oversized glasses. Such was Katy's star power by this stage, that she managed to get a host of celebrities to join her in her homage to the 80s and John Hughes films. It features Debbie Gibson and Corey Feldman (as her parents), Hanson (as the house band), Kenny G (as Uncle Kenny), and *Glee* stars Darren Criss and Kevin McHale. The eight-minute video, starring the character Kathy Beth Terry, is inspired by many of the clichés of 1980s teenage films, including the makeover and an out-of-control teenage party.

"I thought it was really bold of Katy, who is such a sex symbol, to try something like this, but I also knew it would be received very well if done right," said the video's director, Marc Klasfeld, to MTV news. "I worked with Katy on 3OH!3's 'Starstrukk' and knew she could pull off comedy. And she is actually an incredible actress who dove into this Kathy Beth role with reckless abandon. I really hope other artists take Katy's lead and try to not take themselves so seriously all the time. Sometimes, fun can be cool, too."

The video proved hugely popular, the song went to number one, and Katy got her record. The *Teenage Dream* album had five number-one singles on the *Billboard* Mainstream Top 40 chart.

"What a way to wake up! SO proud to announce that the little-engine-that-could of a song 'LAST FRIDAY NIGHT' is officially #1 & made HISTORY!" tweeted Katy. "&u know, I couldn't have done it with out [sic] ya, really I owe u guys BIG . . . so take this moment to give yourself a high FIVE!!! #allbecauseofu." Katy was flying high.

Success story

On July 20, 2011, Katy Perry was rocking out in Seattle with her California Dreams tour, buoyed by the news that she had received the most nominations at the MTV Video Music Awards that year. For the first time, she was up for nine awards, followed by Adele and Kanye West, who were each nominated for seven.

MTV visited Katy in Seattle as part of the live nominations show, and she couldn't contain her glee. "I have nine nominations!" Perry shouted when she heard the good news. "Nine? I thought that was a typo or something! Oh my god, really? Amazing. That's the most nominations I've ever gotten for anything."

Katy was up for Video of the Year and Best Female Video for "Firework"; Best Pop Video for "Last Friday Night (T.G.I.F.)"; and Best Collaboration, Best Art Direction, Best Direction, Best Editing, and Best Special Effects for the Floria Sigismondi–directed "E.T.," which featured fellow nominee Kanye West. "Teenage Dream" also received a nomination for Best Cinematography.

"I'm so excited. I'm nervous like it's my first time," Katy said during the MTV.com live stream, which was broadcasting from backstage as she was getting ready to go out and perform her Seattle concert.

After her show in St. Paul on August 23, Katy took a short hiatus from her tour before heading to Zapopan, Mexico, for a September 1 show. She only had a week off, but it was a week filled with excitement and little relaxation, with the MTV VMAs taking place on August 28, 2011, at the Nokia Theatre in Los Angeles, California.

"It's always exciting to be a part of the VMAs because there's so much spontaneity," Katy told MTV News. "I just remember growing up seeing craziness ensued with the VMAs. I wasn't allowed to see it, but I done watched it!"

Katy and Russell arrived at the awards together—the pair had begun their relationship at the VMAs, after all—and they posed on the red carpet.

Katy picked up a number of awards, giddily making her way to the stage each time. She even collected the top award of the night: a VMA for Video of the Year for "Firework." Upon accepting her prize she said: "I feel like I am doing something right when I sing that song. So thanks to everyone who helped to create it."

Katy also received the award for Best Collaboration for her work with Kanye West on "E.T." After the awards, Katy admitted that she was "just shocked" about her Video of the Year Award "because there's a lot of great people in that category, especially Adele, who I love and is most deserving of anything, any nomination."

"I felt like I was in the right place tonight, especially with that award," she continued. "We all know 'California Gurls' is a great song, but it's not going to change the world or anything like that. But, 'Firework' to me, it feels like it's a movement. I feel like you can always sing songs about clubs and bub and bitches and hos, but it takes a little bit more to sing songs like 'Firework.'"

Unfortunately, there was drama for Katy after the awards. Rumors were flying that her marriage to Russell was falling apart—especially when she attended the post-VMAs House of Hype party at the SLS Hotel in Los Angeles on her own. At that point, no one really believed that the marriage was in trouble, and Katy and Russell denied any marital problems.

Katy continued on her journey. Just one month later, on September 23, she teamed up with Rihanna to open the legendary Rock in Rio music festival in Brazil in front of 100,000 fans. This wasn't any ordinary concert. The fact that she was invited to perform at Rock in Rio proved just how far Katy had come in her career as the show features only big-time musical acts. Her fellow performers included Rihanna, Elton John, the Red Hot Chili Peppers, Metallica, Ke$ha, Shakira, Lenny Kravitz, Coldplay, and Guns N' Roses.

In November 2011, Katy was up for five awards at the EMAs— the European Music Awards held in Belfast. This time, she won Best Live Act, bringing an end to another successful year. However, while everything in Katy's professional life was flying high, her personal life was taking a nosedive.

Opposite: A California–Dreams inspired Barbie doll, complete with cupcakes and Swarovski crystals. Below: Katy in the cupcake dress for European leg of the California Dreams Tour.

"Take advantage of **LIVING IN THE FUTURE** .

We live in an Internet world. Use your **MYSPACE** ;

use your **FACEBOOK** to develop relationships and

a **FAN BASE** . If you have nowhere to play, go

to **OPEN MIC NIGHTS** and sign up. If you want to

learn how to sing better without paying for it, **JOIN THE**

CHOIR! If you want to learn how to play an

INSTRUMENT, teach yourself or **READ A BOOK**

on how to do it. Or trade your skill for someone else's skill.

The answers are **OUT THERE** for you. You just

have to believe in yourself more so than anyone else.

And **DO NOT WAIT** for it to come to you. It will

never come to you, you gotta **GO AND GET IT!** "

D.I.V.O.R.C.E.

Katy had picked up some major nominations and awards in 2011, but, just as she was gearing up for the final performances of her grueling yearlong California Dreams tour, she received a massive shock when Russell filed for divorce, citing "irreconcilable differences," in December.

After the couple didn't spend Christmas together—Katy spent the holiday in Hawaii with friends, while Russell was in London and spotted without his wedding ring—rumors began circulating that their relationship was in trouble.

"Sadly, Katy and I are ending our marriage," Brand said in a statement released to the press. "I'll always adore her and I know we'll remain friends." However, just weeks earlier, Russell had told Ellen DeGeneres that his marriage was going strong and they were "really happily married . . . I'm married to Katy. Perpetually, until death do us part was the pledge. I'm still alive." But, apparently it wasn't going to last that long, as he was the one who filed the divorce papers.

Katy was quiet after the divorce filing—there was no tweeting or interviews. Just silence. However, at the start of 2012, she finally got on Twitter to reach out to her fans: "I am so grateful for all the love and support I've had from people around the world," she wrote. "You guys have made my heart happy again."

Katy had, apparently, been caught by surprise. She'd spent most of the year on the road, which wasn't an ideal way to start married life. Now, as she and Russell went their separate ways, the pair appeared to have settled their separation relatively amicably, swiftly reaching "a written settlement of all issues." However, Katy had to wait until July 1, 2012, before being legally "free," as California has a six-month waiting period for divorces to be final.

Understandably, Katy was too broken to attend the People's Choice Awards, which was held just days after Russell filed the divorce papers. She used Twitter, once again, to inform her fans: "Unfortunately I will not be able to attend the People's Choice Awards. I want to thank u all for voting for me, fingers crossed! #KATYCATS."

Heartbreak aside, Katy still had a tour to complete, though. She packed up her belongings, moved out of her home, and headed for Indonesia for the final leg of her world tour. Katy tweeted: "I'm SO EXCITED to FINALLY be in INDONESIA! U guys have waited forever #timetodeliver."

Tour over, Katy's next major public appearance was at the Grammy Awards in February 2012, where she was nominated for Record of the Year and Best Pop Solo Performance for "Firework." Her performance was highly anticipated. She started off singing "E.T.," but then she surprised everyone as she transitioned into a new song, "Part of Me," which seemed to be

> Katy spent the holiday in Hawaii with *friends*, while Russell was... spotted without his *wedding ring*.

inspired by her recent breakup with Russell. Katy wanted the world to know how she felt, and by the end of the song, no one had any doubts about her ability to move on, as her lyrics revealed her newfound resolve. The song was clearly a final farewell to Russell. Katy was free and back to her old self.

Every time Katy had split up with a man, she had exorcised her pain through her music and created some great tracks. Once more, Katy was using her music as a tool to make it clear to her ex that she had moved on. Soon after the Grammys, the song was released and debuted at number one—Katy's seventh number-one track in her impressive career run.

Katy was back, free, and doing what she did best—continuing to create new songs for her millions of fans across the world.

PICTURE CREDITS

The author and publishers have made every reasonable effort to contact all copyright holders. Any errors that may have occurred are inadvertent and anyone who for any reason has not been contacted is invited to write to the publishers so that a full acknowledgement may be made in subsequent editions of this work. Some of the illustrations in this book have been compiled from more than one original image. This is purely for artistic effect.

SOURCES

Thanks to the following websites for providing information used in the book:

http://artists.letssingit.com/; http://b96.radio.com; http://www.beautylish.com; http://www.billboard.com; http://biographynews1.blogspot.com; http://blog.beliefnet.com; http://blog.mtvasia.com; http://blog.music.aol.com; http://blog.muzu.tv; http://blog.thrillcall.com; http://blog.zap2it.com; http://blogcritics.org; http://blogs.mercurynews.com; http://blogs.tennessean.com; http://bornpowerful.com; http://buzzworthy.mtv.com; http://www.californiality.com; http://celebrity-gossip.net; http://celebs.gather.com; http://celebs.gather.com; http://chartrigger.blogspot.com; http://claytonperry.com; http://www.couturecandy.com; http://www.dailymail.co.uk; http://digitaljournal.com; http://djrossstar-katyperry.buzznet.com; http://en.wikipedia.org/wiki; http://entertainment.ca.msn.com; http://ezinearticles.com; http://www.fabsugar.com; http://fabulousbuzz.com; http://fashion.telegraph.co.uk; http://www.femalefirst.co.uk; http://foreign.peacefmonline.com; http://www.glamourvanity.com; http://guymeetsworld.com; http://www.hitjerker-songwriting.com/; http://hellyeskatyperry.tumblr.com; http://hollywoodcrush.mtv.com; http://www.huffingtonpost.com; http://idolator.com; http://insidetv.ew.com; http://iwillreviewanything.blogspot.com; http://johnanderson.suite101.com; http://justjared.buzznet.com; http://katyperry.buzznet.com; http://katyperry.org; http://katyperry.wikia.com; http://katyperry.unofficialfanpage.com; http://katyperrycaliforniagirls.info; http://katyperryforum.com; http://katyperryspecial.com; http://main.stylelist.com; http://music-mix.ew.com; http://music.uk.msn.com; http://news.softpedia.com; http://newsroom.mtv.com; http://newstweed.com; http://ohnotheydidnt.livejournal.com; http://popwatch.ew.com; http://racketmag.com; http://rapfix.mtv.com; http://seattletimes.nwsource.com; http://steelcloset.com; http://style.mtv.com; http://stylenews.peoplestylewatch.com; http://thelavalizard.com; http://thescotsman.scotsman.com; http://timeline.thefullwiki.org; http://top40.about.com; http://uk.mtvema.com; http://wayback.archive.org; http://wn.com; http://worldidea.net; http://www.accesshollywood.com; http://www.aceshowbiz.com; http://www.allmusic.com; http://www.artistdirect.com; http://www.artistdirect.com; http://www.ascap.com; http://www.beautylish.com; http://www.belfasttelegraph.co.uk; http://www.bellasugar.com; http://www.billboard.biz; http://www.billboard.com; http://www.blender.com; http://www.bokcenter.com; http://www.brits.co.uk; http://www.californiality.com; http://www.cambio.com; http://www.cbsnews.com; http://www.celebitchy.com; http://www.celebstoner.com; http://www.chron.com; http://www.contactmusic.com; http://www.cosmopolitan.com; http://www.couturecandy.com; http://www.dailymotion.com; http://www.dailyrecord.co.uk; http://www.digitaljournal.com; http://www.digitalspy.co.uk; http://www.efb-biosafety.org; http://www.endhereditaryreligion.com; http://www.entertainmentwise.com; http://www.eonline.com; http://www.ew.com; http://www.fabsugar.com; http://www.facebook.com; http://www.femalefirst.co.uk; http://www.fox.com.au; http://www.foxnews.com; http://www.gigwise.com; http://www.glamourvanity.com/katy-perry; http://www.godhatesthemedia.com; http://www.guardian.co.uk; http://www.hark.com; http://www.hitjerker-songwriting.com; http://www.hollywoodlife.com; http://www.hollywoodreporter.com; http://www.hubcapdigital.com; http://www.hulu.com; http://www.hungarybudapestguide.com; http://www.independent.co.uk; http://www.londonderrystandard.com; http://www.mattmcbrien.com; http://www.mercurynews.com; http://www.metrolyrics.com; http://www.monstersandcritics.com; http://www.moron.nl; http://www.mtv.com; http://www.music-news.com; http://www.my9japarty.com; http://www.myspace.com/katyperry; http://www.nme.com; http://www.nowmagazine.co.uk; http://www.npr.org; http://www.nydailynews.com; http://www.nypost.com; http://www.nytimes.com; http://www.ontheredcarpet.com; http://www.people.com; http://www.peoplestylewatch.com; http://www.popjustice.com; http://www.prefixmag.com; http://www.prnewswire.com; http://www.reuters.com; http://www.rollingstone.com; http://www.scotsman.com; http://www.scrappysam.com; http://www.setlist.fm; http://www.sheknows.com; http://www.snakkle.com; http://www.snmag.com; http://www.squidoo.com; http://www.starpulse.com; http://www.startribune.com; http://www.stuff.co.nz; http://style.mtv.com; http://www.sugarscape.com; http://www.theaustralian.com.au; http://www.theaustralian.com.au; http://www.thehollywoodgossip.com; http://www.thehothits.com; http://www.thepulsemag.com; http://www.thestarscoop.com; http://www.thetimes.co.uk; http://www.ticketmaster.com; http://www.time.com; http://www.tmz.com; http://www.ukmix.org; http://www.usatoday.com; http://www.vanityfair.com; http://www.voanews.com; http://www.wearepopslags.com; http://www.womenshealthmag.com; http://worldidea.net; http://www.youtube.com; http://www.zimbio.com